Loneliness, stress and well-being

Loneliness can be a terrible experience and can often contribute to a range of psychological difficulties. Yet, surprisingly, counsellors, therapists and other professional helpers are rarely taught how to help their clients cope with loneliness. Written specially for professional helpers, *Loneliness, Stress and Well-being* provides a thorough background to theories concerning the nature of loneliness and a basic introduction to its management.

The authors, who have extensive experience of treating both interpersonal and psychological difficulties, provide a new hierarchical perspective on the nature of social difficulties and describes a simple method of assessing the degree and nature of the client's loneliness. They provide the helper with practical strategies for helping clients manage their social problems, going beyond the traditional skills training approaches by introducing a multi-level intervention, including thought management and interpersonal problem-solving.

Essential reading for anyone whose clients have difficulties in establishing or maintaining social relationships, the book will be of particular value to counsellors, community nurses, psychologists and social workers.

P.M. Murphy and G.A. Kupshik are both chartered psychologists. They have extensive clinical experience in treating interpersonal and psychological difficulties.

Loneliness, stress and well-being

A helper's guide

P.M. Murphy and G.A. Kupshik

Routledge
Taylor & Francis Group
LONDON AND NEW YORK

First published 1992
by Routledge

2 Park Square, Milton Park, Abingdon, Oxon OX14 4RN
711 Third Avenue, New York, NY 10017, USA

Routledge is an imprint of the Taylor & Francis Group, an informa business

First issued in hardback 2016

Transferred to Digital Printing 2004

Typeset from the author's wordprocessing disks by
NWL Editorial Services, Langport, Somerset

British Library Cataloguing in Publication Data
Murphy, P.M. *1957–*
Loneliness, stress and well-being: a helper's guide.
1. Loneliness
I. title II. Kupshik, G.A. *1959–*
158.2

Library of Congress Cataloging in Publication Data
Murphy, P.M. (Philip Michael), 1957–
Loneliness, stress and well-being: a helper's guide / P.M. Murphy and G.A. Kupshik.
p. cm.
Includes bibliographical references and index.
1. Loneliness. 2. Adjustment (Psychology)
3. counseling.
I. Kupshik, G.A. (Gary Allan), 1959– . II. Title.
III. Title: Loneliness, stress, and well-being.
BF575.L7M87 1991 91–12539
155.92 – dc20 CIP

ISBN 0–415–01450–6 (hbk)
ISBN 0–415–07032–5 (pbk)

ISBN 978-0-415-07032-4 (pbk)
ISBN 978-1-138-16193-1 (hbk)

To friends and family who help us to cope

Contents

Figures and tables

FIGURES

TABLES

Preface

Duncan Cramer

Unlike the common cold, most people claim never to have experienced loneliness. When a representative sample of 9,003 British adults were recently interviewed, 65 per cent said that they had never felt lonely. While 27 per cent admitted to feeling lonely sometimes, only 5 per cent said they had often felt lonely and less than 2 per cent reported that they had always been lonely. However, as pointed out by the authors of this book, people may be reluctant to confess to experiencing a feeling which may portray them in a socially negative light, particularly when talking to a stranger. Consequently, surveys may underestimate the extent of this distressing problem.

Somewhat surprisingly, social scientists have only recently begun to investigate this important issue and our understanding of it is still limited. This book is a welcome step in the direction of furthering knowledge on this subject. The first part provides a conceptual framework for investigating loneliness, drawing upon a broad body of primarily social psychological research and incorporating some original material. One difficulty with discussing emotional experiences such as loneliness, is that the exact nature of the feeling and the conditions under which it occurs need to be known before practical steps can be taken to alleviate it. The second part of the book offers a detailed explication of mainly cognitive-behavioural techniques which can be used to help clients overcome this problem. Since methods of tackling loneliness have received relatively little attention from mental health experts, this section should provide a valuable addition to the armoury of therapists and counsellors.

Part I

Theoretical perspectives

Chapter 1

What is loneliness?
Defining a model

> What is hell – Hell is oneself. Hell is alone, the other figures in it merely projections. There is nothing to escape from and nothing to escape to. One is always alone.
>
> (Eliot 1950, p. 87)

Infernal, lingering, odious void – Eliot's acutely negative note on loneliness. Most people would agree with him that it is an unpleasant experience, but is it really as bad as he implies and if so, does it have any long-term, harmful effects?

In the following chapters we will explore these questions and show that loneliness, in addition to being painful, can actually cause problems in mental and physical health. Then, in Part II, we will give a range of strategies for overcoming loneliness. First, however, we need to know what we mean when we say loneliness. This may seem a simple issue, but it is a very complex experience, and does not easily lend itself to examination. The present chapter, therefore, will dissect loneliness into its more easily understood components. This will give a simple model from which to consider, in subsequent chapters, why loneliness is painful, and how it can undermine health.

ARE THE LONELY DIFFERENT FROM OTHER PEOPLE?

A very broad description of loneliness would be that it involves a sense of deprivation in one's social relationships. This, however, would imply that only lonely people have deficits in their social environments, which is not the case. On the contrary, the majority of people feel that their relationships are a little deficient in one way or another. For instance, a particular friend may be too argumentative, or an employer too demanding, or a spouse not attentive enough. These are all experiences of social deficit, and cause most people to feel a little dissatisfied with their social environment; but it does not make them all say that they are lonely. What, therefore, distinguishes the lonely from those who are not? One obvious answer would be that loneliness is only experienced once the deficit reaches some critical level. However, this makes the assumption that deficits in the environment can increase without consequence until the critical point is reached (whereupon we begin to feel lonely). This is not consistent with people's comments about their experience of loneliness. Few people, for instance, describe the feeling as appearing suddenly, as if some critical point had just been reached.

The problem with the above description is that it tries to dichotomise loneliness, making the assumption that there is a qualitative difference between the experiences of the lonely and those of other people. In other words, it assumes that either a person is lonely or that they are not lonely. Categorising people into these 'either/or' categories is a basic feature of human nature, and has various evolutionary merits. Consider, for example, one of our primitive ancestors out hunting, suddenly confronted with a wild animal; he would not have survived for long if he had paused to decide exactly what kind of animal it was. During such a pause, a dangerous animal would have pounced, or a more defenceless animal, which could have provided essential food, would have escaped. Consequently, to save valuable time, he would instinctively dichotomise the situation, asking himself whether the animal was dangerous or not; and act quickly on the answer (running if it was dangerous, or attacking it for food if it was not dangerous). In this manner, the instinct to dichotomise situations was essential to survival and has, therefore, become central to the way people think.

With loneliness, however, it is useful to resist this temptation to categorise. Instead, it is more appropriate to think in terms of quantative differences, with loneliness simply reflecting the degree of deficit in a person's social environment. For example, someone with no deficits at all would not be lonely, whereas a person with a few deficits would be mildly lonely. Similarly, someone experiencing severe deficits would be extremely lonely. Of course, the feelings experienced will depend on the relationship involved. Deficits in the quality of interaction with a spouse, for instance, will cause greater feelings of loneliness than will problems in a casual relationship. Furthermore, anticipated duration of the current deficit will influence feelings of loneliness. For instance, feeling alone during times of difficulty would be likely to have a much greater effect on feelings of loneliness if a person felt there was no one to help them *at all*, than if they simply felt that there was no one to help them *at the moment*. On the basis of this, Beck and Young (1978) have distinguished between three types of loneliness: chronic loneliness which evolves from social deficits continuing over a period of years; situational loneliness which usually results at the termination of a relationship; and transient loneliness which referred to the short bouts of loneliness that most people experience periodically as a result of brief periods of minor social deficiency.

Clearly, with different relationships and different periods of duration leading to various types of loneliness, it may be more appropriate to think of loneliness in terms of several dimensions rather than as one, single continuum. This is obviously important, and the various dimensions along which social deficits can occur will be discussed in later chapters. For the present, however, it will be more convenient to consider only the net effect of the various types of deficit, by thinking in terms of a single continuum of overall social deficits.

Consistent with the notion of a loneliness continuum, it could be concluded that most people are a little lonely (because we all experience some deficits in our social environment). However, if this is the case, why do relatively few people actually say they are lonely? In order to answer this, it is necessary to consider the opinions they form about themselves when they see that their social environment is deficient.

THE ROLE OF PERSONAL OPINIONS IN THE EXPERIENCE OF LONELINESS

The above description has assumed that there is only a single factor involved in the experience of loneliness: degree of social deficit. However, people do not simply passively observe the things that occur in their social environments. Instead, they are continually contrasting their experiences with those they observe in other people. To do this, they adopt standards or norms by which to judge whether their experiences are typical of those of other people, or whether they are unusual. It is these norms which determine whether a person will call themselves 'lonely'. For instance, having absolutely no friends to talk to might be thought unusual for most people, and be taken as an indication of considerable deficit in their relationships. In other words, the norm would be that people should have friends. Consequently, under most circumstances, a person with no friends would be likely to consider themselves to be lonely. However, the same lack of available conversation would be considered quite normal among monks who had taken a vow of silence. They would, therefore, be less likely to consider themselves to be lonely. Clearly, the relationships of both types of person may be equally deficient, but because of their differing norms, only one would actually refer to themselves as lonely.

In addition to indicating whether people should label themselves as lonely, norms also directly influence their experience of loneliness. In order to understand how this occurs, it is necessary to discuss the process by which sensitivity to norms develops.

THE DEVELOPMENT OF 'NORM' AWARENESS

Although psychologists are not clear about which cognitive faculties a child is born with, it is generally accepted that they are unaware of the complex social norms pervading the world they have just entered. A major school of thought in this context is that a child's development in such areas occurs through a process of learning (see Chapter 2 for further discussion of learning theory). Initially, such learning is provided by the parents as they teach the child some of the more basic norms with which the child will be expected to comply (such as the correct way to eat). During this process, the parent often acts as a model for the child, strongly encouraging it to copy their adult behaviour. Consequently, as time goes by, it strives to become more like its parents; even to the extent of trying to wear their clothes and shoes, and mimicking their gestures and mannerisms. This pattern of encouragement is continued by teachers at school, by other relatives, and by the child's own peers. The child, therefore, copies characteristics of their behaviour also; and, in this manner, develops a belief that to conform to the behaviour of others is 'good', and conversely, that failure to conform is 'bad'.

The strength of the belief that failure to conform is bad has been well demonstrated in a series of experiments conducted by Solomon Asch in the 1950s. He showed that people will even deny the evidence of their own eyes in order to conform. In a typical experiment (Asch 1958) seven people were gathered together in a room ostensibly to participate in a study of perceptual ability. They were told that they would be shown a series of cards displaying three lines of different length and a fourth 'standard' line. Their task was to say which of the three lines was the same length as the standard line. In each case, it was very easy to see which was the correct line. However, of the seven people involved, six (the confederates) had been previously approached by the experimenter and told unanimously to indicate the wrong judgement on some of the trials. The seventh person (the subject), who was unaware that the other six people had been briefed in this manner, would, therefore, be confronted with everyone in the room unanimously agreeing that the wrong line was correct. In this situation, even though it was blatantly obvious that the judgement was incorrect, the subject went along with the opinion of the confederates on about one-third of the occasions. When asked afterwards why they had ignored the evidence of their own eyes, the subject would tend to say that they suspected something was wrong with their eyes. This of course raises the question whether the subject complied because of serious doubts about their eyesight (this would be understandable when faced with so much disagreement). Or were they really conforming so as not to be thought odd by the others? To answer this, Deutsch and Gerard (1955) replicated Asch's study, but allowed subjects to give their answers anonymously. Here, no one could be made to look odd by giving the wrong answers, so the only reason for conforming would be that they doubted their own eyesight. Deutsch and Gerard found that this anonymity greatly reduced conformity. Clearly, therefore, doubts about vision were not sufficient to make people conform. This raises doubts about the explanations given by Asch's subjects, and suggests that it was the lack of anonymity (and subsequent risk of public awareness that they deviated from majority concensus) which forced them to conform.

In parallel to learning that conformity is good and desirable, children also become aware that their social worlds are comprised of distinct groups of people (such as family, school friends, neighbourhood friends, and teachers). Each of these groups have slightly different norms and expectations. For instance, a child's family and teachers may consider it to be a desirable norm for children to work hard at school, whereas the child's friends think otherwise. In the face of these opposing expectations, the child must decide which norm to adopt.

The above dilemmas of choice are encountered frequently through life. Consequently, because people make different choices, they do not all adhere to the same norms. In view of this, individuals often encounter groups of people who have norms (on issues such as fashion etc.) to which they do not conform. This clearly conflicts with the above belief that to be different from others is undesirable, and will, therefore, make them feel 'bad' or 'odd'. Consequently, in order to avoid these negative feelings, the transgressor will try to use one of two coping strategies. They will either try to change their behaviour in order to comply with the new norm, or, strive to vindicate their sense of deviance by justifying their behaviour in terms of allegiance to the norms of some other group. For instance, during the bulk of the twentieth century homosexuality has been severely frowned upon. Consequently, homosexuals have tended to hide their sexual preferences in order to comply with this strong norm of heterosexuality. This was clearly an example of the former strategy of changing (or disguising) behaviour in order to maintain conformity. However, over the past few years a growing number of the gay community have made their feelings public, generating a visible group to which others could identify. This has provided sufficient security to enable increasing numbers of people to openly challenge the norms of society, by freely expressing their sexual preferences. Clearly, because there were now existing social norms which accepted their behaviour, it was possible to choose the latter coping strategy by proclaiming allegiance to this newly visible group.

Whether a person chooses to resist social norms in favour of those of some other group, or to change their behaviour to achieve conformity, will depend upon the degree of deviance of the behaviour, and the strength of their allegiance to the groups advocating the conflicting norms. A problem arises, however, when they fail to comply with a norm, not because of allegiance to some other group, but simply because they are unable to. In this case it is neither possible to justify their deviation from the norm, nor to change their behaviour to comply with the norm. They, therefore, develop the feeling that they are 'different' (perhaps even 'bad' or 'odd'). For example, upon becoming unemployed a person may feel 'different' because they expect that the majority of people they are likely to meet will have jobs. That person is also likely to be aware that having a job is a sign of success, which by definition means that not to have a job signifies failure. Consequently, many of the unemployed are unhappy and dissatisfied (Murphy 1987). Unfortunately, they cannot resist these feelings by proclaiming allegiance to a large united group of other unemployed people who are comfortable with their joblessness, because such a group does not exist. The unemployed person, therefore, cannot justify their unemployment, nor easily change their employment status, but are stuck with their feelings of discomfort.

In a similar vein, a norm stigmatising the lack of adequate relationships is widely held across most social groups (e.g. 'if he hasn't any friends he must be boring or weird'). It is unlikely, therefore, that a person suffering in this manner could avoid the stigma by proclaiming allegiance to some group in which having poor relationships is valued. Furthermore, since friendlessness is often forced upon a person rather than chosen, it would be unlikely that they could improve the content of their relationships. Consequently, as with the above examples, a person with major deficits in their social environment would be unable to avoid feeling socially 'odd', regardless of which groups they identify with.

Social norms, therefore, both indicate when we should begin to consider ourselves to be lonely (i.e. label ourselves as such), and also cause lonely people to feel odd and ashamed. However, sometimes people report feelings of loneliness without exhibiting any apparent shame. Consider, for example, the case of Carl Jackson. In the late 1970s Jackson made a solo voyage across the Atlantic which lasted fifty-one days. After it was completed he said:

> I found the loneliness of the second month almost excruciating, I always thought of myself as self-sufficient, but I found life without people had no meaning. I had a definite need for somebody to talk to, someone real and alive and breathing.
>
> (Jackson 1978)

Jackson clearly had grounds to consider his social environment abnormally deficient at this time. However, this extract appeared in a major American magazine with his approval. It was unlikely therefore, that he considered his loneliness something to be ashamed of. This is contrary to the above conclusions that falling below social norms is always a shameful experience. The reason for this apparent contradiction is that there is one further factor involved in the experience of loneliness which we have not yet discussed. This concerns the *attributions* of blame we make when our needs are not being satisfied, or when we see that we have broken a social norm.

LONELINESS AND THE ATTRIBUTION PROCESS

Psychologists have for many years been interested in how people decide the likely cause of their own and others' behaviour. The study of this process has been termed *attribution theory*. Much of the innovative thinking in this area has been provided by three theorists: Fritz Heider (1944), Jones and Davis (1965), and Harold Kelley (1967). They have suggested that people are interested in understanding the causes of their own and others' actions because it may help them to cope better in future situations. Interestingly, their investigations have shown that when evaluating the cause of other people's conduct, we tend to play down the role of situational factors and exaggerate the role of their personal qualities. For example, when observing that a friend is unusually angry over the course of a day, we are likely to conclude that they 'got out of the wrong side of bed'. In other words, that they are predisposed to get angry with any minor inconvenience, regardless of whether it was actually a 'good day' or not (i.e. that the cause was something inside them). However, when determining the cause of our own behaviour, we are more likely to emphasise the role of situational factors (i.e. we tend not to see the cause as something inside ourselves, but look for explanations around us). Consequently, when we see that we are more angry than is perhaps justified over some issue, we are likely to explain this to ourselves in terms of the things that have happened to us through the day (e.g. 'I've had a bad day'). In a similar vein, people who are not lonely tend to believe that the loneliness of others is a result of personality factors and general appearance (e.g. 'he must be a little strange, or boring'), whereas the lonely are more inclined to perceive their loneliness as being caused by situational factors (e.g. 'it's my work hours' or 'there's just nowhere to meet new people'). Their reasons for doing this have considerable relevance to the experience of loneliness. It will be useful, therefore, to consider the various processes involved. There are three such processes which are most relevant in the context of loneliness: (i) attributional error; (ii) stigma avoidance; and (iii) cognitive dissonance and the need for self- efficacy.

Attributional error

Jones and Nisbett (1972) have suggested that the information available to the person initiating a behaviour (initiator) and those merely observing is essentially different. They point out that the initiator's behaviour is mainly influenced by what they notice in their surroundings. Consequently, when asked to explain what caused such behaviour, the initiator is likely to emphasise features of the situation. The most prominent factor for the observers, however, is likely to be the initiator of the behaviour themselves, because it is the initiator they are watching. They would tend therefore, to explain the initiator's behaviour in terms of their own personal characteristics. The essence of Jones and Nisbett's suggestion is that it is the information most prominent to us that influences our causal judgements. Nisbett and his colleagues tested this idea by asking students to explain why they had chosen their particular college courses, and why they had chosen their present girlfriends. The students were also asked to explain why their friends had made their choices. They found that when explaining their own behaviour, a great many references were made to external factors (e.g. stressing the quality of their course as their reason for selecting it). But when speculating on why their friends had made their decisions, much more emphasis was placed on personal characteristics of the friend in influencing the choice (Nisbett *et al.* 1973).

One consequence of this error of attribution is that persistent loneliness in others has become heavily stigmatised as reflecting major inadequacies in their personalities, such as 'they must be selfish, ugly, or extremely boring'. This means that in addition to having the stigma of being thought odd (because loneliness contravenes social norms), loneliness can also carry with it the stigma of being labelled an inadequate person. The desire to avoid such stigma leads us on to the second attribution process involved in the experience of lonelines.

Need to avoid stigma

It has already been discussed above that through a process of social learning, we develop a strong aversion to appearing odd. In this context, we have discussed how being lonely involves the breaking of social norms and how it can also be seen as reflecting personality inadequacies, both of which promote the sense of being a misfit. This label, however, can be avoided if the cause of the loneliness can be attributed to situational factors. For instance, in the example of Jackson's solo voyage, it is clearly apparent that his loneliness was not a result of his personal characteristics. Instead, it was caused by the socially barren nature of the environment he endured. In view of this, personal stigma about the loneliness could not be attributed to him. Consequently he would have no reason to hide the fact of his loneliness. There are likely to be many reasons why situational explanations remove the stigma in this manner. However, one major consideration is that it indicates the deviance is not an enduring characteristic of the person, but an unfortunate (and usually temporary) result of their circumstances.

Cognitive dissonance and the need for self-efficacy

Through observations of how psychiatric patients overcome their difficulties, Bandura (1977) has concluded that the belief that one has personal mastery over the environment has an essential role in effective daily functioning. He suggests that when faced with difficulties, this belief in self-efficacy encourages people to be more willing to attempt a solution and also promotes greater persistence. Consequently, in view of its adaptive qualities, people continually search for evidence of their efficacy. For instance, both Langer and Roth (1975), and Wortman (1975) have shown that people frequently inappropriately attribute their successes to their own ability, thereby bolstering their confidence.

When a person feels lonely the implication is that they do not have sufficient mastery to provide for their social needs. This generates a condition called 'cognitive dissonance'. The notion of cognitive dissonance was first introduced by Leon Festinger in 1957. A 'cognition' is a generic term used to refer to a person's thoughts, beliefs, values, and attitudes. The basis of Festinger's theory was that people desire to maintain consistency among their cognitions. For instance, it is commonly accepted that smoking is harmful to health. Consequently, people who still smoke will experience cognitive dissonance because the fact that they smoke (indicating their approval of the habit) is inconsistent with their knowledge that it is harmful. In order to resolve the dissonance, it would be necessary for them to change one of the two cognitions to bring it into consistency with the other. This is clearly observable in the ingenious ways smokers convince themselves that it is all right for them to smoke.

Subsequent revisions of the theory have pointed out that dissonance only occurs when at least one of the cognitions involved is of importance to the individual (Brehm and Cohen 1962). Consequently, someone who does not smoke may quite happily hold the two conflicting beliefs that it is all right to smoke and that smoking is harmful, because neither of these cognitions are particularly important to him. However, when important cognitions are involved, dissonance is unpleasant and actively avoided (for further discussions on the unpleasantness associated with cognitive dissonance see Jones and Gerard 1967; Wicklund and Brehm 1976).

Returning now to the above comments that being lonely implies failure to achieve adequate personal mastery, we have already pointed out that people have a strong desire for personal-efficacy. Being lonely is not consistent with this important cognition. Consequently, the individual experiences cognitive dissonance. By explaining their loneliness in terms of unavoidable aspects of their environment, the loneliness ceases to undermine the need for efficacy, thereby restoring cognitive consistency. However, if they cannot blame the environment in this manner (perhaps because they are largely responsible for their loneliness), they will have to find some other method of dealing with the dissonance. The only remaining options are either to admit to themselves that they do not have personal-efficacy (which will of course considerably undermine their self-esteem), or to remain in a state of cognitive dissonance. Both of these alternatives will clearly be unpleasant.

If a person, therefore, is forced to attribute the cause of their loneliness to themselves, they will feel stigmatised, a failure, and often in a state of cognitive dissonance. Clearly, these factors must be considered when attempting to understand the experience of loneliness.

SUMMARY

It is not sufficient simply to dichotomise loneliness. People should not be categorised as being either lonely or not lonely, but instead, be considered in terms of degree of loneliness, with all people placed somewhere between the two extremes of the loneliness continuum (i.e. 'not lonely at all' to 'extremely lonely'). The basis of a person's position on this continuum is, in part, the degree of social deficit they are experiencing. However, in addition to this, their feelings are also influenced by fears that, because they have broken norms, others will see them as odd, subsequently labelling them as 'lonely people'. This will be exacerbated by feelings of failure, inadequacy, and cognitive dissonance, if the norm breaking cannot be attributed to factors other than themselves (pushing them further into feelings of loneliness). The combined contributions of these three factors (social deficits, social norms, and attributions of responsibility) are given in Figure 1.

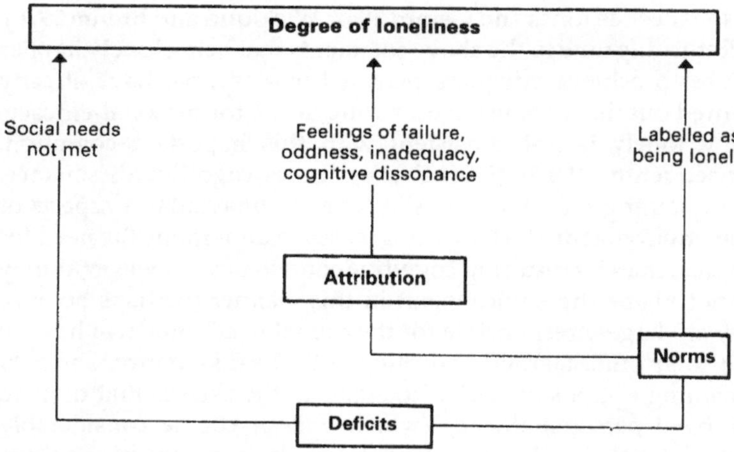

Figure 1 Three factor model of loneliness.

Chapter 2

Why people need people

In Chapter 1, it became clear that social norms and social attribution can serve to exacerbate the feelings of distress caused by a deficient social environment. But what is a deficient social environment? A common belief in this context is that a simple reduction in the number of people we have contact with will promote feelings of loneliness. For example, the *Oxford Dictionary* defines lonely as:

> Lonely: Solitary, companionless, isolated; unfrequented; *sad because without friends or company.*
>
> (Sykes 1982)

Indeed, it is often the case that being alone does cause a person to feel lonely. Remember Carl Jackson's solitary voyage across the Atlantic described in the previous chapter. However, it would be wrong to assume that this is all loneliness is; merely a reflection of the number of people we have contact with. Even in the lives of Britain's national celebrities, for example, despite their popularity and frequent social revelry, loneliness is still a common experience (*The Times* 1983). Furthermore, there are accounts of many people through history who have shunned contact with people almost totally, without exhibiting any of the accompanying pains of loneliness that might be expected. St Anthony, for instance, chose to spend twenty years in isolation on the banks of the Nile, apparently without any desire for company (Anson 1932). Another recluse was even recorded to say:

> I relish the charms of solitude more and more and am trying to find out how to enter into deeper and deeper solitude.
>
> (Anson 1932)

Of course, very few people actually choose to live in such isolation, and it is important to remember that most people who spend their time alone do so because they are unable to 'mix-in' with others. However, it is clear that what causes one person to crave company, may not have the same effect on another. What is it that causes these differences? To answer this we must examine what is gained from social interaction, thereby discovering what people want company for.

WHAT IS GAINED FROM SOCIAL INTERACTION?

Various psychological theories have been employed to address this question, each concerning different aspects of people's social needs. It is not possible to consider them all, but some of the more popular approaches include attachment theory, need for approval, social comparison, need for practical help, and learning theory. There is considerable overlap between these various approaches, with many of them involving common concepts such as self-esteem and social compliance. Nevertheless, it is simple for the moment to think of them as being distinct. Therefore, each will be individually discussed in the following pages.

Attachment theory

Perhaps one of the most fundamental relationships from which to begin a discussion of social needs, is that between an infant and its parents. Attachment theory concerns the special relationship (or bond) which develops between them, and traces its effects on the subsequent social needs of the child throughout its life. As soon as a child discovers it can crawl, it begins to follow its mother from room to room, being content to play only when it feels assured that she is present. This desire for the presence of the parent is reflected throughout the animal world. Monkeys cling to their mother; calves and lambs, if separated, will cry endlessly until their mother locates them. Bowlby (1973, 1980) has studied the parent/child relationship extensively. He showed that a child's desire to maintain close proximity to its parents during certain stages of its infancy is so strong, that if suddenly separated even for a short while it will become considerably distressed, refusing to be consoled or looked after by anyone else.

On the whole it is the mother with whom the infant establishes the greatest attachment. However, this is not because of any unique biological bond between them. In a review of research in the area, Rudolph Schaffer (1980) has pointed out that the infant will in fact establish attachment with any person who takes the mother's role at an early age. Furthermore, if several people take on the role of the mother, it is capable of forming multiple attachments with all of them (although the involvement of too many people may serve to confuse it).

Bowlby (1973) has provided detailed accounts of the changes which occur in the parent/child relationship as the child ages. He showed that as it grows older the child develops an increasing tolerance for separation from its parents. It becomes content to play in their absence, and, by school age can be separated from them for many hours without signs of distress. This does not, however, signify a reduction in the need for attachment. On the contrary, in part, it merely reflects the child's growing desire to play and explore further and further afield. Driven by this desire to explore, the child (while continually checking that its caretaker is there) begins to play around the room they occupy. It soon learns that simply being out of their presence does not mean that it has been abandoned, which eventually gives it the confidence to play out of their sight in different rooms. In this manner, the child develops increasing confidence that absence does not imply abandonment, which enables it (as it grows older) to play outside and away from the home. Clearly therefore, in this context, the increased tolerance for separation does not indicate that the child no longer needs attachment, but that it develops confidence in the permanance of its current relationships.

Another reason why the child becomes more tolerant of separation is that it begins to develop alternative attachment relationships, which reduce the role of the parents as the only source of attachment. For instance, children frequently have a 'best friend' or special groups of friends or 'gangs'.

The need for attachment then, continues through childhood with only the source of gratification being changed. In fact, the tendency to establish attachments is continued throughout life. For instance, in adulthood the attachment feelings are typically directed towards someone with whom adult life may be shared. The similarity of these adult attachments with those of the child to its parents has been well illustrated in a series of interviews documented by Weiss (1975). He quotes one thirty-year-old woman who had been recently separated from her husband, for example, as saying:

> When my husband left I had this panicky feeling which was out of proportion to what was really happening. I was afraid I was being abandoned. I couldn't shake the feeling.
>
> (Weiss 1975, pp. 49)

Her anguish clearly has similarities to Bowlby's observations of the unconsolable distress of a child when it feels abandoned by its parent.

An adult's need for attachment has been further emphasised by studies of the recently bereaved. Such studies have often found that people who have just lost a spouse will attempt to satisfy their need for attachment by establishing a compensatory relationship with one or more of their children. One woman, for instance, explained that her relationship with her eldest son had reached the point where, 'When he went into the service' . . . 'I missed him more than I missed my husband' (Weiss 1979, pp. 88). Alternatively, people strive to replace their lost attachment through relationships with other relatives and friends, or seek out new compensatory relationships. In one instance, for example, a woman pointed out when describing her separation from her husband: 'Immediately after we broke up I threw myself into a relationship with somebody else' (Weiss 1975, pp. 67).

These behaviours do not mean that a spouse or co-habiting partner is essential. Many people, for instance, never co-habit in this manner, choosing instead to satisfy their need for attachment solely through friends and relatives. However, whatever means are chosen to satisfy the need, termination of the relationship is reflected by a strong desire to find alternative sources of attachment.

The above examples show that from infancy to adulthood people strive to form close attachments with other people, but why do they do it? Initially, it was believed that the desire by infants for parental proximity developed because the parents were perceived as the major sources of gratification for its basic practical needs (such as for food). However, this was not consistent with some of the observations of animals. For instance, ducks feed themselves from birth, negating their parents as a source of need gratification. Nevertheless, they continue to have a desperate need to maintain proximity with a parent, spending a large proportion of their early days following their mother about. Similarly with human infants, the intensity of parental attachment is not influenced by whether the parents are reliable, loving, or caring of the child's health and welfare. In fact, even in cases where the child is frequently beaten, abused, and deprived, they still often exhibit a strong attachment to the parents (Rutter 1972). The pattern is the same with adult-to-adult relationships. For example, Weiss, who has held many interviews with couples who are at the point of separation, indicated that:

> Even when marriages turn bad and the other components of love fade or turn into their opposites, attachment is likely to remain. The spouses resemble battered children in their feelings: they may be angry, even furious, with one another; they may hate one another for past injuries and fear one another's next outburst of rage; after a quarrel they may find consolation in fantasies of confrontation and revenge in which they imagine themselves saying, 'You can just take your things and get out of here' or 'Don't try to find me because I'm not coming back.' But when they actually consider leaving their marriage they become almost paralyzed with fear.
>
> (Weiss 1975, pp. 44)

Even the binding force that offspring establish between their parents cannot account for this parental need to stay together, because Weiss (1975) showed that similar feelings can occur between husband and wife even when the children have left home. In spite, therefore, of little apparent benefit, people are still anxious about breaking attachments.

Clearly then, the desire for attachment is not simply explained by a wish to be close to those who provide for personal needs. Of course, people do tend to spend much of their time in the company of those who satisfy their needs. Consequently, it is not surprising that it is them with whom close attachments are usually established. Nevertheless, even when the needs are no longer being satisfied (and are even being undermined), the desire for attachment persists – but why do people desire these attachments?

One factor likely to go some way to answering this question is a simple need for company. It would be inappropriate to assume that this could account fully for the phenomenon because when abandoned by an attachment figure, the company of others is not always comforting. Nevertheless, it does appear to be involved and this becomes most noticeable when people are afraid. For example, a classic experiment demonstrating this aspect of human nature was conducted by Schachter in 1959. In his experiment, subjects were informed that they were about to receive several electric shocks. Half of them were made to feel fearful by being told that the shocks would be painful; the remaining half were not frightened, but were told instead that the shocks would be very mild and that they would enjoy them. Both groups of subjects were subsequently infomed that they would have to wait for ten minutes before the experiment began, and that they could either wait alone or with other people. Schachter found that although some of the unfearful group wanted to wait with other people, almost twice as many of the frightened subjects preferred company. As previously, this desire for company did not simply reflect an expectation that something would be gained from the others (such as words of reassurance). Further studies, for example, have found that the preference for company existed even when the subjects were not allowed to talk to those with whom they waited (Firestone *et al.* 1973).

Mere company, however, is not an adequate substitute for attachment. Consequently, as the need for comfort increases beyond the mild feelings promoted by Schachter's experiments, people search for intimacy rather than solely for company. For instance, while living with a rifle company in the Korean War, the sociologist Roger Little studied the behaviour of soldiers in the unit. Among his observations he pointed out that fear increased the need for closeness. Consequently, 'the longer the unit was 'on the line' directly confronting the enemy, the more intense their relationships became (Little 1964, pp. 213).

In summary, therefore, the need for attachment, rather than reflecting a simple need for general company, seems to be more concerned with intimate company (usually, as Weiss's evidence shows, with only specific individuals at any one time). Furthermore, attachments are often formed when there is no apparent gain for the individual; and considerable distress is experienced at their termination, even when maintaining the attachment means enduring an unpleasant relationship. These observations serve only to obscure further the reason why people seek and maintain attachments. Of course there are clear survival merits in maintaining close proximity between a vulnerable infant and its parents. Consequently, the need for attachment may simply reflect an adaptive biological drive which has evolved to protect the species. In this context, adult attachment needs could be viewed as the free-floating remains of this drive once the benefits of parental proximity were out-grown. This is, however, speculation and no relevant biological mechanism has been identified which could account for this. Therefore, firm conclusions regarding the motivation for attachment must remain the subject of future investigation. Nevertheless, regardless of why the need exists, attachment clearly constitutes a major component of people's social needs. Consequently, failure to achieve it will contribute significantly to the experience of loneliness.

Before proceeding to discuss the various other theories about why people need social interaction, there is an issue arising from attachment theory which could usefully be discussed at this point: 'Are close relationships more important than casual relationships?'

Close versus casual interaction

One of the conclusions outlined above is that people have a strong desire for close, intimate interaction (reminiscent of being with parents during childhood). On the basis of this conclusion, some researchers (e.g. Henderson *et al.* 1981) have suggested that people need only close, intimate interaction to help maintain their feelings of well-being, and that casual types of interaction are relatively unimportant. Whether or not this is the case is clearly pertinent to understanding the nature of the deficits likely to promote loneliness. It will be useful, therefore, to discuss it in some depth.

Consider first the evidence arising from attachment theory itself. The above investigations have only shown that close interaction is desirable; not that it is more important than casual interaction. Contrary, therefore, to Henderson's suggestions, attachment theory does not imply that casual interactions are unimportant. However, two other sources of evidence have been provided as supporting the notion that close interactions are more important than less intimate interaction. These involve ideas concerning (i) social investment and (ii) bereavement and loss.

(i) Social investment

Several investigators have observed that people invest more effort in maintaining close relationships than they do in casual ones (Rosenblatt 1977; Rusbult 1980). It would seem logical to assume, therefore, that the former were more important. However, let us examine the issue more closely, and ask why people invest time and effort in close relationships. One major reason is that these relationships are often used to share intimate problems (not necessarily guarded secrets, but more often personal views, opinions, and anxieties). However, people are reluctant to disclose too much about themselves for fear that the information may become public knowledge, leaving them feeling vulnerably open, or that the listener may mock or reject them. Consequently, the process of disclosure is typically slow and cautious. This pattern of cautious self-disclosure is known as social penetration (Altman and Taylor 1973), because the process of getting to know someone intimately is like penetrating a social onion, where first we restrict them to the superficial outer layers of ourselves, permitting them to proceed deeper only when we feel sure they can be trusted. For example, in the initial stages of a developing close relationship, each partner continually monitors the trustworthiness of the other, while at the same time offering tokens of their own dependability by making small disclosures. These disclosures may be nothing more than statements of preference about harmless issues interspersed within more general conversation, but in this manner growing trust develops within the relationship, and over time disclosures become more significant. Also, as additional tokens of commitment, we are likely to defend the name of our close friends when they are criticised by others. Similarly, we tend to be more giving of both practical and emotional help and support.

On the basis of people's willingness to commit so much effort to close reationships, and the relative lack of effort invested into sustaining casual relationships, it can be argued that the former must be more important than the latter. For example, with casual relationships (such as those with most work colleagues, local shopkeepers, and neighbours), although investing some minimal efforts into being polite, people are unlikely to invest much effort in defending the name of such people if they are criticised by others. Neither is it so likely that they will be offered practical or emotional help. These differences in social investment, therefore, do appear to support Henderson's ideas. However, to invest more disclosure in a casual relationship would effectively change the nature of the relationship such that it became more intimate (Kelley *et al.* 1983, pp. 299–300). Consequently, if one is to retain a casual relationship as casual, it is necessary that too much disclosure does not occur.

So it may be wrong to assume instead that we can't be bothered to invest disclosure and acts of intimacy in our casual relationships, but that we actively avoid doing so to ensure that we do have some casual relationships. Indeed, sometimes, by inadvertently disclosing too much within a relationship (common between the sexes when mildly intoxicated), an otherwise pleasantly casual relationship can become more intimate than the members would have preferred – which often leads to the total dissolution of the relationship. If close relationships were, as Henderson suggests, important to the exclusion of casual relationships, such incidences would not be a problem because we would want to make all of our relationships intimate.

(ii) Bereavement and loss

Henderson has used as evidence for his argument the fact that people express greater concern at the forced ending of a highly intimate relationship than occurs with casual relationships (Henderson *et al.* 1981, pp. 35). Clearly, this does seem to suggest greater importance of intimate relationships, but there are other explanations. For instance, the greater distress of people losing an intimate relationship may result not from a greater need for intimate interaction, but because they perceive that it will be a long time (if ever) before they will be able to establish a replacement relationship (because of the demanding criteria involved, such as high mutual trust). The loss of a casual relationship, however, is less worrying because they are relatively easy to replace. In other words, close and casual relationships may both be important, but it is harder to replace the close ones. Of course, a further reason for the greater distress when losing intimate relationships is that they often occur through painful divorce or death, whereas casual relationships are more likely to change because of less significant factors such as moving neighbourhoods.

A more detailed analysis of the specific interactions people need will be made in the Appendix, contrasting both casual and intimate components, and further conclusions will be drawn regarding this issue. However, for the present it is clear that caution should be exhibited when making assumptions about the respective merits of close and casual interaction.

Need for approval

Returning now to our review of the various theories for why people seek relationships. Some investigators have suggested that need for approval is a major factor which promotes this search for interaction. Researchers have observed that most people are sensitive to the opinions others have of them, preferring that their views are positive. For example, Dittes (1959) found that students became negative and despondent if they believed that others didn't care for them. Similarly, Jones and Schneider (1968) showed that such people were considerably relieved when they subsequently found that others did value them. In view of this need to be approved of, people chosen as friends and partners are typically those who provide us with positive evaluations. Coombs (1969), for example, showed that among over 200 computer-dated couples, those eager for further dates were typically pairs where partners had been openly approving of each other, of the things they did, their beliefs and ideals, their ambitions (or lack of ambitions), their interests, the way they dressed, and the style of life they led. This was also the case among couples where partners did not seem to notice each other's foibles, or the things that emphasised their inadequacies. Of course, it is rare that one encounters many people who would approve of all of these things, and it would be unrealistic to abandon a relationship simply because they had begun to disapprove of something we had done. Nevertheless, it seems clear that whenever possible, people strive to include within their relationships only those who show approval of them.

This need for approval has been interpreted by researchers as reflecting a more basic need to maintain a positive self-view, or self-esteem (Crowne and Marlowe 1964). Clearly, continual disapproval from others would lead a person increasingly to doubt themselves, causing their self-view to become more negative. Searching for approval therefore, can be viewed as an attempt to defend and protect self-esteem. Consistent with this conclusion,

Gecas (1971) has found that people whose self-esteem was low (i.e. they did not think very highly of themselves) searched more actively for approval than those with a higher self-esteem.

Exactly why people have this need to maintain a positive self-view is not understood. Nevertheless, it clearly provides a strong drive to seek the company of others, failure in which leaves the individual without any means of affirming their sense of self-value, thereby causing them to feel negative and despondent.

Social comparison

Throughout life people continually ask themselves questions about the things they encounter from one day to another. Many of these questions are easily answered; for example, what day is it, and what time will the next bus arrive? However, some present considerable difficulty: should chemical weapons and nuclear bombs be banned; does God exist; who should be the next prime minister? These questions are not easily answered because the issues involved are rarely clear, and there is no right or wrong answer. Consequently, people are faced with perpetual uncertainity about their world and the issues within it. Festinger (1957) has suggested that people resolve this uncertainty by comparing their views with others. Clearly, the more people that agree with a person's opinion, the more secure they can feel that their view is correct. Festinger pointed out that when confronted with disagreement, the individual may either change their own opinion, persuade others to change theirs, or decide that the others are irrelevant as comparison persons (e.g. dismiss them with the thought, 'they're fools anyway').

People generally prefer not to have to change their opinions. This is partly due to reluctance about having to think the whole issue through again, but a more important reason is that many of these ideas become central to the way we view ourselves and the world. George Kelly pioneered and wrote extensively on this matter in the late 1950s. Unfortunately, it is beyond the scope of this book even to begin seriously to describe his ideas here (the reader is therefore referred to Liebert and Spiegler's (1974) review of his work). Summarising his work, however, Kelly pointed out that many of our attitudes and opinions are so central to the way we function as individuals, that to change them would undermine our overall pattern of thinking. Consequently, people prefer to interact with others who are likely to share and support their views.

A further reason for maintaining a favourable social comparison is to sustain a positive self-esteem. Clearly, to find oneself in frequent disagreement with others is likely to mean continual re-assessment of one's own beliefs. This will bring with it the likelihood of ridicule by one's peers, and a growing sense of inadequacy regarding one's own opinion formation skills. In the face of this, it would be hard to maintain any kind of positive self-esteem.

Additionally, concerns about being seen as odd (i.e. non-conforming, as discussed in Chapter 1) are also likely to promote the need for social comparison, so that we can obtain continual reassurance that we are not 'odd' but are just like everyone else.

So strong is our need to compare favourably, that our whole decision making process can sometimes be undermined by other people. This has been strikingly illustrated in a wealth of experimental studies. Typical of these was Latané and Darley's (1968) investigation in which students were invited to what was ostensibly an interview. As they sat in a waiting room smoke began to pour through an air vent in the room. In this situation, 75 per cent of the students who waited alone reported the smoke quite quickly. However, on some occasions a student was asked to wait in a full waiting room, where, unknown to him, all the other people in the room had been previously told to ignore the smoke. In this situation less than 16 per cent of students reported the smoke, even when the room was completely filled. Blatant evidence was discounted (or explained away) in favour of the apparently more widely held opinion in the room that there was no danger. This finding has been even more strikingly demonstrated in a study by Latané and Rodin (1969) where, instead of smoke, subjects heard a female in the next office (separated from them by only a curtain) fall while she was standing on a chair. She yelled 'Oh my God, my foot' and then continued to groan for about a minute. Once again significantly more of the subjects who were waiting alone came to her aid.

The costs of our need for favourable social comparison, therefore, can be high, requiring us to relinquish at times much of our independence in decision making. Nevertheless, the gains such as increased self-esteem, and increased certainty regarding the unpredictable factors inherent in daily life, seem to compensate, thereby causing us actively to seek the company of others.

Practical help

A further reason for wishing to be in the presence of other people is to ensure that help is available when we need it. In this context, research has shown that both humans and animals become physiologically aroused when they observe another's suffering and that the greater the suffering, the greater the arousal (Gaertner and Dovidio 1977). Furthermore, several studies have shown that the higher the arousal, the faster the subsequent help (Gaertner and Dovidio 1977; Geer and Jarmecky 1973; Krebs 1975). This suggests that people have an innate biological drive to behave altruistically to others in distress. Such a drive would mean that should a person need help, it would always be available if they were with other people. This, by providing a clear (albeit an unconscious) motive for seeking the company of other people, would help explain why people do not like to be alone for too long. However, altruism is not always observed in reality, which somewhat undermines this conclusion. For example, one evening in 1964 in a respectable neighbourhood in New York a psychopathic murderer took half an hour to kill Kitty Genovese, leaving and returning three times to finish her off (reported in Berkowitz 1980). She screamed repeatedly while being murdered, yet although thirty-eight of her neighbours had witnessed the event from their windows, none called the police.

The case of Kitty Genovese clearly seems contrary to the above evidence that people are pre-disposed to help, but perhaps they didn't realise help was needed? This relates back to the previous section on social comparison. Brown (1986), for example, points out that neighbour's reports showed that they all assumed others had gone to investigate; and as no police had arrived, concluded that nothing serious was occurring (maybe she was an actress practising her script). Of course, there are other reasons why people ignore pleas for help. Over-exposure for example can desensitise people to the suffering of others. This type of response can frequently be seen in major cities, where drunks and beggars are by-passed and ignored. Additionally, concerns for their own safety would cause a person to think twice before going to investigate groans coming from a dark, isolated alley. However, these cases involve relative strangers; within established relationships (friendships etc.) the drive to help is stronger. In part, this is because greater knowledge of the person removes the type of uncertainty that may have prevailed around the Genovese incident. Consequently, there is less room for doubt about whether help is really needed. However, in addition to this, it would be likely that their approval was valued (as discussed earlier in this chapter), and this would be jeopardised by ignoring their requests for help.

It is possible to conclude two things from this brief review of the altruism literature. First, that although various factors may prevent altruism, people do have a strong pre-disposition to help others. Secondly, that greater likelihood of help is available within established relationships. This clearly provides a strong motive for seeking company, especially to establish stable and ongoing relationships.

Learning theory

Learning mechanisms also provide explanations for why people seek company. Unfortunately, however, to do justice to a discussion of learning theory is beyond the scope of this book (for more thorough coverage the reader is referred to Hilgard *et al.* 1979). Nevertheless, it is a major contender among the factors promoting the need for social interaction, and therefore warrants consideration here. In its simplest 'classical' form (Pavlov 1927), learning theory suggests that when a person has an identical pleasant (or unpleasant) experience on several occasions, then any other experiences occurring simultaneously on these occasions will be tainted by the experiences. For example, when given a mild unexpected shock, a person is likely to feel startled. Now, if (repeatedly) at the same time as receiving each of the shocks, they heard a soft buzzer, the buzzer would become associated with the shock. Consequently, if at some later time they heard the buzzer without the shock, they would still give the same startled response (even if they had been forewarned that there would be no shock). What has happened is that they have learned to become alarmed by a buzzer which previously had no effect on them. Many theorists believe that this process of learning to be alarmed is exactly how phobias develop (review by Garfield and Bergin 1978).

Learning theory contributes a significant explanation for why we seek the company of others. For example, throughout childhood, a child's parents care for and nurture it. In this context, the presence of people becomes associated with comfort and pleasure, so that eventually, even at times when they are not providing care or nurturance, their very presence becomes comforting and pleasurable (in much the same way as the buzzer became associated with unpleasant shocks). Similarly, when a child hurts itself, its mother (or some other caretaker) soon comes to provide help. In this manner, the mother becomes associated with the removal of pain and fear, and her absence makes the child feel insecure and vulnerable; so the child ensures that she is never far away. As the years pass, this security generalises to other people who have similar characteristics to the mother (i.e. are caring, comforting, and nurturing). In this manner, the individual learns to find comfort in the presence of such people, and, if deprived of such relationships, will begin to feel vulnerable and insecure. This is not to say that people are continually searching for mother substitutes, but that through their childhood the expression of caring in others became associated with security, and that in order to maintain the feeling of security they now strive to be with people who care for them. Of course, not all people's experiences are quite like this, consequently some people shun caring behaviour in others (sometimes because of unpleasant parent figures in childhood). It is also important to note that although most of the development in this context does occur in childhood, a great deal of learning goes on throughout life, continually changing the nature of a person's social needs.

Midlarsky and Bryan (1967) have found that learning experiences also encourage the expression of altruistic behaviour. People therefore learn to enjoy exhibiting a degree of altruism, which provides additional motivation for their seeking social interaction. In this manner, a wide range of social norms are learned. Learning theory therefore, provides considerable insight both into why people seek social contact, and why within these relationships they prefer some forms of interaction over others.

LEVELS OF SOCIAL NEED

So far in this chapter, we have discussed various needs which cause people to seek social interaction. These needs have a hierarchical structure. For instance, consider the following: the need for approval; the need to compare favourably with others; and the need to maintain high self-esteem. Needs of approval and for favourable social comparison are both, in part, important because failure to achieve them would undermine a person's self-esteem. This means that the primary social need (or most important social need) among the three is the maintenance of self-esteem, with the other two merely being the means by which this is achieved (i.e. secondary social needs).[1] Figure 2 lists various primary and secondary needs, and, below them, some of the interactions (or social resources) which can be used to satisfy them.[2] The model given is not exhaustive and there is a need for much research before the exact hierarchies of need are understood. For example, some primary needs may collectively contribute to some even more basic needs or drives (sexual needs and security needs, for instance, are both at least partial reflections of the most basic drive for survival of self and race). Conversely, some secondary needs may be represented by more peripheral tertiary needs.

The distinction between primary and secondary needs is not merely semantic, but has considerable relevance for understanding why people feel lonely. For instance, without the categories it is not possible to draw any conclusions about the degree of loneliness caused by impoverished social environments. This can easily be illustrated with the examples given in Figure 2. For instance, it cannot be assumed that a person will feel lonely simply because their need for attachment and need to compare well with others are not being satisfied. On the contrary, such feelings will depend on whether these deficits have a significant effect on their primary needs; which will depend on the degree to which other related secondary needs are being met. For example, returning to Figure 2, if a person is enjoying a great deal of approval from others, then attachment and social comparison will play a less significant role in maintaining their respective primary needs (i.e. self-esteem and a sense of security). Consequently, deprivation of these two secondary needs will only have a minor effect on feelings of loneliness. However, if the person does not feel approved of by others, then deprivation of attachment and favourable social comparison will be much more likely to undermine their primary needs for self-esteem and security and thereby lead to greater feelings of loneliness.

Similarly, it is not possible to make any assumptions about how lonely a person should feel simply by observing the social resources available within their environment. The ability of any of

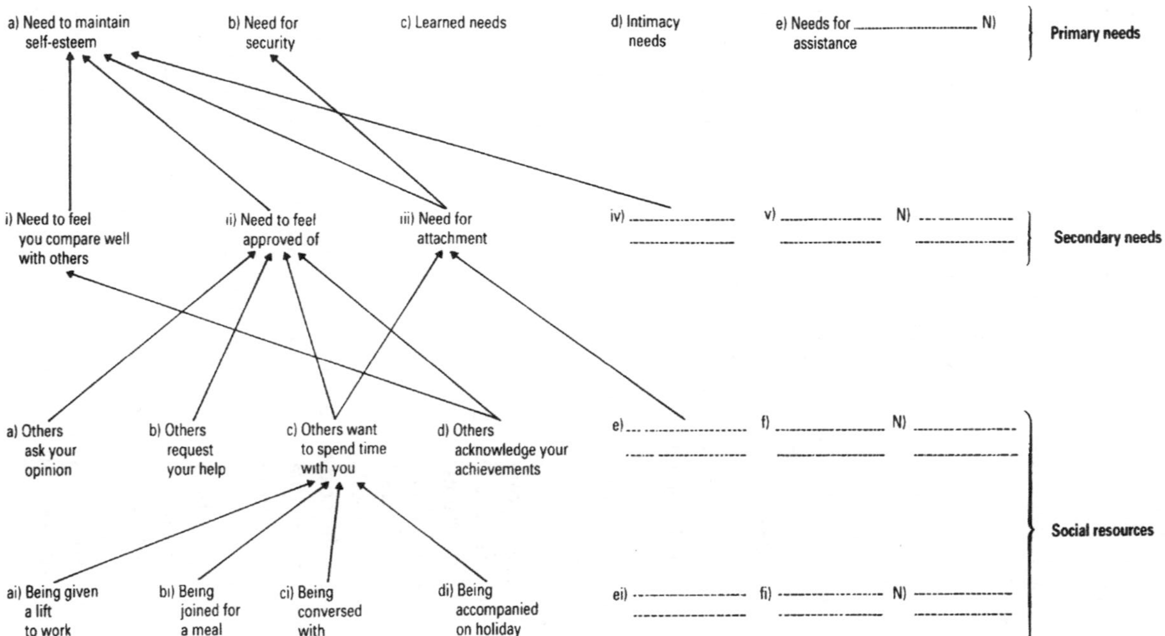

Figure 2 Sample of the hierarchy of social needs and its resources (showing some primary needs, secondary needs, and social resources, and some of the relations amongst them).

the available resources to satisfy primary needs will depend very much on which secondary needs have been prioritised. This can be graphically illustrated in the early life of a university student, and answers the question 'why do some students become lonely in spite of tremendous social resources available within the student environment?'. Of course, one explanation for their loneliness might be that they simply do not 'mix-in' easily with others. However, although this is often the case, it would not provide a complete account because many students who seek help for loneliness frequently describe having had perfectly normal social behaviour prior to entering university. Why then do they feel lonely? The answer to this is likely to lie in the social resources available within their new 'university' environment. Many students, for example, before entering university will have been among the most academically able members of their school. This will have satisfied their secondary need to feel they compare well with others, thereby satisfying the primary need of maintaining self-esteem (Figure 2). However, upon entering university, since everyone cannot be 'the best', many students find that they are no longer among the most able students, but are merely one among many of similar competence. This considerably reduces the support for their self-esteem. Furthermore, while at home, it is likely that their parents would have been strong sources of approval through displays of parental praise and pride in their success. This, as above, means that before entering university their self-esteem was receiving considerable support. Most students, however, leave home when they go to university, which would effectively sever this source of approval.

Going to university, therefore, brings with it the threat of a major loss in self-esteem. Consequently, in order to re-establish their favourable social comparison (and with it improve their self-esteem), they sometimes have the option of using other skills as the basis for comparison (e.g. musical, or athletic ability) which might enable them, once again, to compare well with others. Unfortunately, this is not a viable alternative for most students. Therefore, they must seek to increase their self-esteem via some other secondary need, such as obtaining approval. Typically, they soon identify peer groups with interests similar to their own (universities are renowned for their great wealth of clubs, societies, parties, and discos). This provides an opportunity to meet people who will want to spend time with them, and to communicate with them. These interactions indicate approval (Figure 2) and thereby help to re-establish and maintain their self-esteem.

In some cases, however, a student does not choose this approach. Instead, rather than trying to restore their self-esteem through the approval of others, they may try to do it by re-building their favourable academic social comparison (often by working much harder, sometimes even confining themselves to their rooms). In other words, they choose to *prioritise* social comparison rather than approval as their means of restoring self-esteem. It is this type of student who is inclined to subsequently seek help for loneliness. The reason for this, as we have discussed, is that the need to maintain self-esteem is only one among many primary social needs; the other needs, therefore, will be being deprived while they spend so much time working alone. As a result of this, they may eventually decide to compromise by working a little less often and instead try to involve themselves more with others. Unfortunately, by this time most of the other new students will have already established stable peer groups, which are not immediately receptive to intrusion by new members. In view of this, attempts to interact more fully with others may not be successful. In addition, therefore, to having low self-esteem and worries about their academic competence, they would now also feel deprived of other primary social needs, and also feel a little rejected by other students.

Why some students should try to restore their self-esteem in this manner, by excessive study causing them to ignore peers, is open to question. Their past experiences may have shown it sometimes to be an effective method of dealing with such problems. Or perhaps other pressures (such as the insistent 'encouragement' to do well by parents) make increased socialisation seem a less suitable method of restoring self-esteem than hard work. The example is, of course, highly simplistic. In reality, people do not prioritise only a single secondary need, but are more likely to give graded preference to various such needs, depending on past experiences and current desires. Nevertheless, it is clear that their personal decisions (i.e. which secondary needs they are prioritising – in this case social approval or social comparison) considerably influence the usefulness, and sometimes accessibility, of many of the social resources within the environment.

USING THE HIERARCHY OF SOCIAL NEEDS TO OVERCOME LONELINESS

We have asked the question in this chapter, 'what is the nature of the social deficits which cause loneliness?' Not surprisingly, in answering this, it has become apparent that the need for social interaction is caused by a range of psychological phenomena which give rise to a wealth of social needs, interlinked by a complicated hierarchical network (Figure 2). Consequently, overcoming loneliness is not a simple matter of increasing one's company. Instead, it involves the difficult tasks of:

(task 1) finding out which primary needs are not being met.
(task 2) then, in trying to meet these deprived needs, finding out which secondary needs the person is able to utilise.

Achieving task 2 is not simple and presents a considerable hurdle to those who would help people overcome their loneliness (we will discuss this further in Part II of this book). Dealing with task 1, however, seems much more simple. It would appear that we merely need to construct a single, complete hierarchy of all needs and resources. Then, using this as a chart, observe which social resources were lacking in a person's social environment, and then plot which secondary and subsequently primary needs were not being met. If it was found for instance (referring to Figure 2), that a person's friends never asked for their help, never praised them, or never really wanted to spend time with them, we might conclude that they were experiencing social deficits which undermined their need for approval, and were therefore likely to be suffering from a low self-esteem. However, there is a significant problem with this strategy. It assumes that people essentially have the same needs. And that although circumstances can sometimes restrict the usefulness of some social resources, generally all people can use the same resources to satisfy a particular need. In the following chapter it will be shown that these assumptions are unsound, and that caution must be exercised if the hierarchy of social needs is to be used as a basis for assessing and overcoming loneliness.

NOTES

1 Readers familiar with Maslow's (1954) hierarchy of needs should be careful not to confuse his with the present hierarchy. Malsow's needs were relatively distinct, with each level of the hierarchy only being engaged once needs from lower levels had been satisfied. However, in the present case, the levels of need are highly interdependent and the satisfaction of needs at a lower level (secondary needs) directly affects satisfaction of needs at higher levels (primary needs).

2 Not all needs and resources have been included, neither have all of the potential links between them. To have included more at this point would have been confusing and obscured the issues being illustrated.

Chapter 3

Inter-personal and intra-personal differences in social needs

In Chapter 2 some of the social needs which cause people to seek company were described. If these needs were the same for all individuals, determining what is causing someone's loneliness would be a relatively simple matter. Unfortunately, however, large differences can be found between people. This is most noticeable when the needs of different cultures are compared, but marked differences can also be found in the needs of people from the same culture, and, even the social needs of a single person change from time to time. We will begin by looking at the cultural differences.

THE CHANGING NATURE OF SOCIAL NEEDS – ACROSS CULTURES

America has been the focus of most of the research into social needs. Let us consider first, therefore, a typical example of this research, and then compare the findings with those of other societies. Weiss (1974) has found that Americans desire six basic factors from their social environments:

1 *Attachment* is provided by relationships from which participants gain a sense of security and place. In the presence of attachment-providing relationships individuals feel comfortable and at home.
2 *Social integration* is provided by relationships in which participants share concerns, or even better, by a network of such relationships. Membership in a network of common-concern relationships permits the development of pooled information and ideas and a shared interpretation of experience. It provides, in addition, a source of companionship and opportunities for

exchange of services, especially in the area of common interest. The network offers a base for social events and happenings, for social engagement and social activity.

3 *Opportunity for nurturance* is provided by relationships in which the adult (. . . or young person . . .) takes responsibility for the well-being of a child and so can develop a sense of being needed. Responsibility for children seems to provide meaning to an individual's life and to sustain commitment to goals in a wide variety of activities.

4 *Reassurance of worth* is provided by relationships which attest to an individual's competence in a social role. Colleague relationships function in this way for some men (. . . and women . . .), particularly for men (. . . and women . . .) whose work is difficult or highly valued. Relationships within the family may function in this way for other men (. . . and women . . .) for whom a sense of competence depends not on particular skills, but rather on their ability to support the family.

5 *A sense of reliable alliance* is provided primarily by kin. Only within kin ties, especially those between siblings or lineal kin, can one expect continuing assistance whether there is mutual affection or not. We would surmise that individuals cut off from their families, or without familial relationships, would feel constantly limited to their own resources and at times vulnerable and abandoned.

6 *The obtaining of guidance* seems to be important to individuals when they are in stressful situations. At such times it seems important for individuals to have access to a relationship with an apparently trustworthy and authoritative figure who can furnish them with emotional support and assist them in formulating and sustaining a line of action (author's brackets) (Weiss 1974; pp. 23–4).

Weiss found these needs to be important across all of the Americans he interviewed. They are not, however, shared by all cultures. Consider, for example, the need to nurture children (point no 3). Some societies exhibit a relative distaste for this activity. Levy (1973), for instance, observed that in the Tahitian culture a large majority of children were given away at birth to other members of the community. This was done as a token of friendship and regard, to bind otherwise unrelated families. Once established in their adoptive home, the children were strongly discouraged from exhibiting any dependency behaviour towards the new parents. Initially a baby would be pampered and cared for as much as any Western child, but by the time it reached about three years old, serious 'adult type' behaviour was expected from it. People would begin to react to it in an adult way, perceiving 'dependency, helplessness, and regression to childlike behaviours ... as profoundly disturbing, dangerous, and valueless' (Levy 1973, pp. 26). To illustrate this discouragement of childlike dependency, Levy gave the example of a young boy (approximately five years old) called Etienne:

> Etienne discovered that his sisters had been given gifts by a visiting European, but that none had been given to him. He began acting 'unusually', became irritable, made himself a nuisance, and got in the way of the play of other children. He began to knock over small pieces of wood and toys that the girls were playing with. He then picked up a pair of scissors and began making stabbing motions at his sisters. He then began to cut off pieces of his own hair with the scissors. None of the older siblings or adults sitting around paid any visible attention at all to Etienne's behaviour.
>
> (Levy 1973; pp. 446–7)

This sudden transition from nurtured child to independent youngster represented a major crisis for such children, causing them to cling in babylike ways, trying to reassure themselves that their elders were still concerned about them. Nevertheless, in spite of their requests for assurance, the children were simply 'brushed off' (Levy 1973, pp. 455). This behaviour is not unique to Tahitians. Goldschmidt (1975), for instance, was struck by the apathy Sebi parents (a Southern Nilotic tribe of Uganda) exhibited towards their children's needs, pains, and suffering. Clearly, therefore, not all cultures share the desire, which Weiss found among his American interviewees, to feel needed by their children.

Other studies have indicated similar cross-cultural disparities. For example, the desire to have a confidant with whom to share problems has been noted in both American (Sisenwein 1964) and Dutch surveys (Jong-Gierveld 1984). However, this need is not found in all cultures. McGoldrick (1982), for instance, while studying the social mores of the Irish, noted that they were very reluctant to talk about their problems and suffering even to close family members, and often became confused and embarrassed when encouraged to do so. Similarly, Midelfort and Midelfort (1982), who had spent a considerable time working with Norwegians, also observed a marked reluctance to disclose problems to others:

> Norwegians believe that they should not burden their family or even their closest friend with personal problems or feelings of inadequacy.... Friendship is demonstrated through loyalty over time and by spending time together not by sharing intimate problems. Family and friends are united by a silent understanding that life is hard and made more worthwhile by this loyalty and steadfastness.
>
> (Midelfort and Midelfort 1982, pp. 443)

Further evidence of the cultural differences in social needs has been found by Murphy, *et al.* (1989). The study was designed to identify which aspects of a relationship were felt to be most important by British people. The results showed that what was important depended on the type of relationship in question (Table 1). Consequently, for example, although respondents felt it was important that an intimate partner should show concern about their problems (Table 1 item 19), this was not so important with casual friends (Table 1, items 1–7). This clearly has implications for understanding loneliness, which will be discussed in later chapters. Returning for the moment, however, to the current issue of cross-cultural differences, we can compare the list from the British respondents with that described earlier from Weiss's research with American respondents, which reveals a marked similarity between them. For instance, items 2, 13, 23, 34, and 39 (Table 1) are clearly important if a person is to be reassured of their value (Weiss's item 4). This similarity would, of course, be expected in two cultures as socially, economically, and technologically alike as Britain and America. Nevertheless, even between cultures this similar, major differences can be observed. For example, items reflecting Weiss's 'need for guidance' (point no. 6) did not appear among the forty British items. Additionally, items 9, 10, and 16, on the British list, which collectively involved a concern by respondents with their public image as a spouse, and items 25 and 31, which referred to the adjustment of their children, did not have counterparts on Weiss's list.

Table 1 List of social factors which British people consider important in providing a satisfactory relationship

Important with my friends	1	Whether they want me to stand by them in times of trouble.
	2	Whether they think I will stand by them in times of trouble.
	3	Whether they are willing to stand by me in times of trouble.
	4	How loyal they are to me.
	5	How honest they expect me to be with them.
	6	How honest they are with me.
	7	Whether they break promises they have made to me.
Important with my intimate partner	8	How honest they think I am.
	9	Whether they have a good opinion of me.
	10	How confidential they keep the things they know about me.
	11	Whether they say (or do) things which worry or concern me.
	12	How much they respect my privacy.
	13	How much time they like to spend with me.
	14	How well they expect me to keep my promises to them.
	15	Whether they break promises to me.
	16	Whether I sexually satisfy them.
	17	Whether they sexually satisfy me.
	18	How honest they are with me.
	19	How much concern they show when they hear about my problems.
	20	How loyal they think I am to them.
	21	How well they appreciate me.
	22	Whether they will stand by me in times of trouble.
Important with my children	23	Their opinion of me.
	24	Whether they think I have a good opinion of them.
	25	How good or bad they are morally.
	26	How hurt they are when I have to make harsh comments about them.
	27	How often they are physically ill.
	28	Whether they want me to stand by them in times of trouble.
	29	Whether they think I will stand by them in times of trouble.
	30	Whether they are willing to stand by me in times of trouble.
	31	Whether they have psychological problems.
	32	Whether they want to turn to me in their times of need.

continued

Table 1 (cont.)

	33	Whether they expect me to stand up and defend what I believe in.
	34	How much respect they show me.
	35	How honest they are with me.
	36	Whether they break promises to me.
	37	How much they respect my right to my views.
	38	Whether they think I want to respect their privacy.
Important with my parents	39	Their opinion of me.
	40	How often they are physically ill.

Reprinted from: Murphy, Summerfield, & Watson (1989)

THE CHANGING NATURE OF SOCIAL NEEDS – WITHIN CULTURES

The above brief review of the research into people's social needs shows explicitly that there are major variations in the needs of different cultures. This complicates considerably the task of understanding the causes of a person's loneliness. Unfortunately, the problem is compounded further by the observation that even individuals from the same culture exhibit different expectations of their relationships. A major controversy in this context concerns the needs of the sexes. Reviewing the literature on social needs, Reisman (1981) drew the tentative conclusion that there was a sex difference in what was needed from a relationship (pp. 216–18). Women, for example, tended to emphasise the importance of intimacy, and of confiding interactions. Men, on the other hand, were more interested in shared activities and 'having fun'. This is supported in part by the findings of Miller and Ingham (1976) which showed that only women appeared to exhibit signs of distress when there was a deficit of close, confiding relationships, but both men and women were distressed when there was a general lack of acquaintances (presumably, women in this condition experienced distress through lack of confiding acquaintances, whereas men were distressed through lack of shared activity). However, the main support for Reisman's suggestions was the finding that generally women tended to be more lonely than men (Weiss 1973), despite the fact that women were increasingly moving into similar social roles as men. The argument here was that because the social environments of the sexes were becoming increasingly similar, only a difference in social needs could really explain Weiss's findings.

The evidence in favour of Reisman's views was clearly considerable. Nevertheless, Borys and Perlman (1985) have challenged his conclusions by suggesting that the sex distinction had occurred merely because 'women were more apt than men to label themselves as lonely' (p. 4). They argued that during the process of assessment, investigators had tended to make it blatantly clear that it was loneliness which was being assessed. Consequently, because men tend to hide their loneliness, it should be expected that women would appear to be more lonely. They went on to show that when assessment procedures strived to hide the fact that loneliness was being assessed, men were actually found to be more lonely than women. There was, however, a serious limitation in their evidence. They based their conclusions on a review of twenty-eight studies, the bulk of which had used the University of California at Los Angeles (UCLA) loneliness scale. During the development of this scale it was assumed that men and women had the same social requirements (Russell *et al.* 1978). This is unfortunate because many of its items in the scale emphasise intimacy and closeness (items 2, 5, 7, 8, 12, 13, 15, and 20; Table 2), whereas only two concern shared activity (1 and 9; Table 2). This emphasis means that, if Reisman's conclusions (that only women are really concerned with intimacy and closeness) were correct, the scale may not be asking the appropriate questions to measure men's loneliness. Furthermore it would be encouraging men to score more negatively (i.e. more lonely) than women. For instance, if men are less interested in intimate social experiences, they would be likely to establish fewer close, confiding relationships than women. Consequently, it would be expected that an instrument like the UCLA scale, which basically measures prevalence of intimate experiences, would indicate greater deficits for men. This would not, however, reflect greater loneliness, because the men would be unconcerned by the deficit.[1]

Of course, whether the sexes do actually have different social needs, and whether women really prefer more intimate, confiding interactions than men, will remain unresolved until further research clarifies the issue. Nevertheless, even if there was no sex difference, the problem of understanding how lonely a person

Table 2 Questions comprising the UCLA loneliness scale

1	I am unhappy at doing so many things alone.
2	I have nobody to talk to.
3	I cannot tolerate being so alone.
4	I lack companionship.
5	I feel as if nobody really understands me.
6	I find myself waiting for people to call or write.
7	There is no one I can turn to.
8	I am no longer close to anyone.
9	My interests and ideas are not shared by those around me.
10	I feel left out.
11	I feel completely alone.
12	I am unable to reach out and communicate with those around me.
13	My social relationships are superficial.
14	I feel starved for company.
15	No one really knows me well.
16	I feel isolated from others.
17	I am unhappy at being so withdrawn.
18	It is difficult for me to make friends.
19	I feel shut out and excluded by others.
20	People are around me but not with me.

Reprinted from: Russell *et al.* (1978) pp. 291–292

feels remains difficult. This is because even individual people fail to exhibit a consistent pattern of social needs. For instance, Dickens and Perlman (1981) have shown that, at times, having friends takes on considerable importance, and is crucial to a person's emotional adjustment. Reisman (1981), on the other hand, has shown that at other times friendships are much less important, and are treated with almost casual interest. In a similar vein, most people experience periodic fluctuations and changes in their other social needs. Simply thinking back over one's own recent social experiences, for example, will show a range of situations where needs seem to have changed. Perhaps on one day you felt lonely and wanted company, or to visit some friends. On another day, however, you may have preferred to be alone. Likewise, at times we desire quiet, intimate conversation, and at others loud, boisterous activity.

Clearly, the tendency for social needs to differ across cultures, between sexes, and particularly for each person from time to time, makes it very difficult to understand what a person might need to overcome their loneliness. It is important therefore to know why the differences are occurring.

CAUSES OF CULTURAL, SUB-CULTURAL, AND INTRA-PERSONAL DIFFERENCES IN SOCIAL NEED

Reisman's suggestions, which we discussed earlier, that the sexes have different social needs, may seem to imply that biological factors caused the differences. This however, is unlikely to be the case because Money *et al.* (1955) have shown that children who have accidently been reared as the wrong sex (usually because of a physical deformity which hides their true sex) frequently adopt all of the attitudes and preferences typical of the sex to which they have been crossed (although Stoller (1968) has shown that this is not always the case). If their social preferences were biologically determined this would not have occurred, and they would have continued to exhibit their 'natural' behaviours.

A further limitation with the biological argument is that it cannot account adequately for all of the differences in social needs which were noted in the previous section. For instance, throughout history there has been considerable migration and subsequent inter-marriage between Americans, British, and Irish, which must have considerably diluted any biological differences between them. Yet despite this, we have seen above that there are still considerable differences in their social needs. Furthermore, no biological mechanisms have been found between cultures or between sexes which could account for the differing social needs. In view of this, there seems little point in pursuing a biological basis for the differences. It would seem prudent, therefore, to look for other factors which might provide an explanation.

One such precipitating factor concerns not differences in the basic social needs themselves, but in the social resources by which they are satisfied. For instance, it was noted in Chapter 2 that one of the reasons people seek the company of others is to maintain their own feelings of esteem and value. In other words, interaction is merely a resource people use to maintain their self-esteem (and to meet their various other needs (Figure 2)). However, as a result of social norm differences, an interaction which promotes self-esteem in one country may not do the same in another country. Consequently, although promoted by the same need to maintain self-esteem, the kind of interaction people seek will vary from culture to culture. One well-documented example of this concerns cultural differences in preferred 'social distance'.

However, before examining the cultural differences here, let us first consider very briefly what is meant by 'social distance'. Social distance theory (or proxemics) was pioneered by Edward Hall (1966) who showed that people were very sensitive to the distances between them. He found that there were strong rules about how close people could stand to one another, and that breaking the rules (by standing too close) could give rise to anger and hostility. Subsequent investigators have found that a great deal could be inferred about the relationship between two people, merely from observing the average distance between them (the social distance) as they spent time together. Mehrabian (1969), for example, noted that the more people liked each other, the closer they tended to stand together. Similarly, Rosenfeld (cited in Somer 1969) found that when two people were in conversation, they would stand closer together if they valued each other's opinions. Clearly, therefore, if people keep their distance from a person, it is likely to undermine that person's self-esteem by making them feel that they do not like that person, and do not value their opinions.

Returning now to our discussion of cross-cultural effects, a question raised by social distance theory is how close must people stand in order to feel valued. In answering this, research has shown that the size of these preferred distances varies considerably between nations. For example, Little (1968) investigated interaction differences across five cultures (American, Scottish, Swedish, Italian, and Greek) and found that Greeks preferred to be over 30 per cent closer to one another than did the Scottish. Similarly, Hall contrasted the preferred distances between Americans and Arabs, and found that Arabs chose to stand so close to their friends that they could smell each other's breath. Americans, on the other hand, preferred distances which did not allow this exchange. The consequence was that, when in America, Arabs often became confused because people would not stand close enough to them. They would ask themselves 'do I smell bad' or 'are they afraid of me' (Hall 1966 p. 150) and, as a result, they would 'feel socially and sensorially deprived and long to be back where there is human warmth and contact' (p. 148). Clearly, therefore, although promoted by the same need to bolster feelings of self-esteem, social distance norms caused a difference in the social requirements of the two cultures, with Arabs (unlike Americans) requiring sufficient closeness to smell the breath of others.

There are also social norms which actually present a barrier to people satisfying some needs at all. For example, it was pointed out above that the Irish and Norwegians (unlike other cultures) do not seek a confidant. This, however, does not mean that they do not wish to have a confidant, but simply that their social norms prevent them from having one. McGoldrick (1982), for instance, has pointed out that norms inherent in Irish religious beliefs dictate that virtue lies in silent suffering, and that to complain or seek the help of another is to fail. Similarly, Norwegians believe that suffering is either a punishment for sins or a test of their faith (Midelfort and Midelfort 1982), and that to be a valued person they must bear their difficulties alone. These strong social norms present a considerable barrier to satisfying the need to share problems with others. It does not, however, mean that the Irish and Norwegians suffer a silent agony. Instead, they may have found other ways of dealing with their burdens. For example, Zola (1966) and Zborowski (1969) found that the Irish have developed a considerably higher tolerance of pain than other cultures. Furthermore, they have developed a style of humour which helps reduce the stress of personal life-crises, thereby reducing their need to seek help. McGoldrick illustrates this remarkable humour through Böll's (1967) comparison of German and Irish responses to crises:

> When something happens to you in Germany, when you miss a train, break a leg, go bankrupt, we say: it couldn't have been any worse; whatever happens is always the worst. With the Irish it is almost the opposite; if you break a leg, miss a train, go bankrupt, they say: it could be worse. Instead of a leg you might have broken your neck, instead of a train you might have missed heaven, and instead of going bankrupt you might have lost your peace of mind, and going bankrupt is no reason for all that.... With us ... [the Germans] ..., it seems to me, when something happens, our sense of humor and imagination desert us; in Ireland that is just when they come into play.
>
> (McGoldrick 1982, p. 320)

Whether these methods actually compensate for the lack of a confidant has not been investigated. However, Kelleher (1972) has shown that the Irish, who avoid sharing their problems with others, do not exhibit the psychological problems commonly observed in other people who are deprived of such interactions (e.g. care eliciting disorders such as psychosomatic or hypochondriacal symptoms). This suggests that the coping strategies of the Irish are effective. When cultures are unable to adapt in this manner, however, the norms can lead to considerable pain. For example, we described earlier Levy's (1973) and Goldschmidt's (1975) observations that Tahitian and Sebi cultures do not permit dependency behaviour in young children. It is hard to see how the children in such societies could adapt to this. It is not surprising therefore, that, as Levy points out, they suffer considerably because of this norm and strive quite hard in their earlier years to re-instate warm nurturance from their parents.

Although the existence of these restrictive norms explains why some of the differences in social behaviour exist, it cannot explain why the sex differences noted by Reisman occur. Here, unlike social distance, and unlike dependency in offspring, the difference is not just one of degree, with one of the sexes, for example, preferring closer proximity than the other, or less dependency from their children. Instead, there is an actual difference in the types of interactions preferred (men preferring shared activity, and women preferring intimate disclosure). Norms will clearly be involved here, because social attitudes in many Western cultures actively discourage too much intimate disclosure among men. Nevertheless, if the sexes had the same needs, it would be expected that men would feel deprived because of this normative pressure to avoid disclosure. Reisman's evidence suggests that this is not the case, and that men actually prefer less disclosure.

One potential explanation for why the sex difference occurs lies in Money and his colleagues' (1955) observations of children reared as the wrong sex. As we have discussed earlier in this chapter, these children learned to adopt the needs of the sexes to which they have been crossed. It would seem reasonable to surmise, therefore, because they *learned* sex appropriate needs in this manner, that this is how normal males and females develop their needs. In other words, the sexes *learn* to need the interactions defined by Reisman (very much in the style described in Chapter 2).

Clearly then, some differences in the needs of cultures and subcultures are likely to occur, not because norms restrict their expression, but because the respective cultures actually promote the learning of new social needs. A further example can be seen in the British culture. McGill and Pearce (1982), for instance, studied the social value system of British immigrants in America, contrasting them with other cultures, and concluded that their norms were heavily preoccupied with success. This influenced everything they became involved in, even their relationships. Consequently, once a relationship was seriously undertaken (such as in marriage), the goal of being a successful partner became of primary importance. So strong was this commitment to success that marriage was often viewed as 'a contractual relationship' and 'if a spouse fails to perform adequately sexually, to earn enough money, or to provide enough security, he or she has not kept the bargain. (McGill and Pearce 1982, p. 466). This pre-occupation with success was also reflected in the child rearing relationship. British children were expected to be principled, responsible, and self-reliant; lack of demonstration of which was indicative of considerable failure for the parent. These culturally specific contractual requirements of the marriage relationship, and expectations of successful child rearing, are consistent with some of the observed differences in the social requirements of the British and Americans. Namely, that the former have a particular concern (not observed among the latter) with their public image as a spouse and also with the adjustment of their child (e.g. Table 1, items 9, 10, 16, 25, and 31 respectively). Clearly, therefore, these differences represent needs arising specifically and directly from prevailing cultural norms.

Not all variations in social need, however, can be explained in terms of the above normative and learning processes. We have discussed earlier in this chapter, for example, how even the needs of a single person will change from time to time. Neither the prevailing social norms, nor the influences of learning processes can easily explain this. Most cultural norms, for example, tend to be relatively stable, changing only slowly over the course of many years. Similarly, learning is typically slow, following a developmental pattern. The social needs of a single person, however, as we have described, can change backwards and forwards from moment to moment and day to day.

Of course, some of the changes in a person's social needs do occur systematically over the years, and can be explained in terms of changing norms and developmental learning. Consider, for example, the differing friendship needs of teenagers and adults. Teenagers, faced with turbulent changes in their concepts of self, morality, and autonomy, develop special needs of friendship:

> The support and security of the peer group provide adolescents with the opportunity to work through new aggressive and erotic feelings often associated with psychological changes through puberty. [also] the adolescent turns to the peer group to learn the acceptable norm for behaviour in the changing adolescent sub-culture. [Furthermore] as the child increasingly disengages from the family s/he needs the intimacy that friendships provide to compensate for the loss of intimacy in the family relationship.
>
> (Dickens and Perlman 1981, p. 104)

In adulthood however, needs change, and with them the quantity and nature of friendships sought. Reisman (1981) for example, reviewing various studies of adult social relationships, concluded:

> Friendship is an important social relationship throughout adulthood [but] for many adults it is relatively less important than marital or family and career considerations. For males, friends appear to be valued as companions who share mutually enjoyable activities and pastimes. For females, friends appear to be valued primarily as confidantes.
>
> (Reisman 1981; pp. 219)

Nevertheless, we must look beyond learning and norms to explain the day-to-day fluctuations in a person's social needs. We have, of course, provided some explanation for the phenomenon in Chapter 2 when discussing the way people frequently change their prioritisation of the various secondary needs. In addition to this, a person's current experiences may temporarily increase their desire to satisfy a specific primary need, thereby changing the relative benefit provided by different interactions. For example, if someone has recently been severely humiliated, their need for interactions which boost their self-esteem may be greater than at other times. Consequently, whereas minimal approval from others may normally suffice, they may become quite lonely for a while if their sudden need for esteem-enhancing solace is not satisfied. In other words, returning to our needs hierarchy given in Figure 2, a threat to their primary need to maintain their self-esteem caused them to prioritise the secondary need for company and approval.

Apparently sudden changes in a person's needs are not, therefore, indicative of major changes in their need hierarchy, but merely changes regarding which items within the hierarchy are currently of most importance to them.

In conclusion, a person's hierarchy of social needs is very dependent on their culture, sex, learning experiences, and the current life stresses they are facing. These factors influence primary needs, secondary needs, and can also restrict the social resourses available to meet the various needs. As a consequence, great caution should be shown when making any assumptions about what a person needs, what is making them feel lonely, and what may help them overcome their loneliness.

NOTE

1 Borys and Perlman's inappropriate use of studies involving the UCLA scale emphasizes the importance when measuring loneliness, of ensuring that careful consideration is given to whom is being assessed. This issue will be covered in greater detail in Chapter 6 when discussing methods of measuring loneliness.

Chapter 4

Loneliness and social support theory

Loneliness has been linked very strongly with poor psychological health. Research seems to indicate that not only is loneliness an unpleasant experience, but that it is also deterimental to well-being. If this is the case, then the job of helping people overcome their loneliness takes on new significance. It is important to clarify therefore, exactly how much effect loneliness has on health.

Much of the work in this area has concerned 'social support' not loneliness, but essentially, loneliness and social support are very closely related. Investigators, however, have tended to hold them distinct, considering them to be unrelated phenomena. This makes it difficult to discuss the health-related consequences of loneliness without generating considerable confusion. The present chapter, therefore, will explore the relationship between the two concepts. First, we will discuss the origin of the term 'social support' and the various definitions which have subsequently appeared in the literature. Then, having achieved a clear idea of what is meant by the term, we will contrast it with the ideas about loneliness which we have developed through the preceding chapters. This will reveal that there is, in fact, very little difference between the two concepts, thereby providing a clear forum in the subsequent chapter (Chapter 5) to discuss the effects of loneliness on well-being.

SOCIAL SUPPORT

In order to understand the origin of the term social support, it is first necessary to have some understanding of the term 'life events'. A great number of positive correlations have been found between the stressful experiences currently occurring in a person's life, and their physical and psychological well-being: tuberculosis (Hawkins *et al.* 1957); cancer (Solomon 1969); blood pressure (Goldberg *et al.* 1980); heart disease (Jenkins 1976); schizophrenia (Jacobs and Myers 1976); depression (Brown and Harris 1978). These include events such as a change in role for the subject (job loss, marriage), a change in role for another family member (husband off work because of a strike), major changes in health, residence changes, goal fulfilment or goal frustration, and isolated dramatic events such as witnessing an accident, or being stopped by the police (Brown and Harris 1978, p. 67). All of these experiences promote stress, and results have indicated that the greater the number of such events currently occurring in a person's life, the greater their vulnerability to the type of problems outlined above.

The link between health and life events presented an enigma, because most people's lives were full of such events, but very few seemed to become ill as a result. To resolve this puzzle, Hinkle and Wolff (1957; 1958) conducted a series of studies to investigate the role of various cultural and social factors in mediating the vulnerability to stressful events. The results of their work indicated the importance of social relationships in helping people to cope with life events; which marked a turning point in much of the research into life events, and raised the question 'how do relationships help people to cope?'. In a review of subsequent studies, Cassel (1974) proposed that the beneficial role of social relationships is best understood in terms of the presence of supporting factors within them. In other words, he simply stated that many social experiences were able to support well-being. Stimulated by this idea, a great deal of research has been carried out (see review by Cohen and Syme 1984) attempting to identify which social experiences could support well-being[1] in this manner and how they achieved it. Cassel's ideas about their mode of functioning was that they buffered people from the harmful consequences of life events; but other research suggested that social supports were likely to maintain well-being through different mechanisms (the various mechanisms proposed will be discussed in Chapter 5). Nevertheless, what was significant about Cassel's ideas were not his suggested mechanisms, but that he had identified social supports as a key topic for investigation, thereby providing a common focus for otherwise disparate models.

Defining social support

Since Cassel coined the term social support, there have been various developmental changes regarding its definition. However, before proceeding to review them below, it would be helpful to address a contentious issue concerning which aspects of social experience are being referred to when we speak of social supports. Basically, social experience can be broken down into three components:

1. The source of the interaction (peer groups, family, employers, strangers).
2. The social interaction itself, or the social experiences which result from the interaction.
3. The cognitive consequences of the interaction or experience (increased self-esteem, increased feelings of security).

Each of these will be involved in the amount and type of social support being experienced by an individual, but they are all distinct factors. To a large extent it is unimportant what each is called, but it is clearly necessary for conceptual clarity that some distinction is maintained between them. Unfortunately, this has not been the case. For example, Kessler *et al.* (1985) has referred to the sources of social interaction (the types and number of relationships held) as social support; whereas Kahn and Antonucci (1980) considered the resulting interactions and social experiences to be the actual supports. However, contrary to both of these suggestions, Cobb (1976) pointed out emphatically that only the cognitive consequences of these social interactions and experiences could truly be referred to as social supports. Of course, it is unimportant which is referred to as the social supports because each is inseparable from the others (for example, for any social experience there must be a source, an interaction, and a cognitive consequence). Nevertheless, in order to maintain clarity, the following terms which have been most prominent in the relevant literature will be adopted through the following chapters:

Social networks/ ties/contacts:	These terms will be used to refer to the various sources of social support.
Social supports:	This term will be used to refer to those social experiences which promote psychological well-being.

Supported cognitive processes: This term will be used to refer to the beneficial cognitive changes which result from social support.

Continuing now with the developmental changes in the investigation of and definition of social support. Some definitions have been too vague to be useful. For example, Kaplan (1975) defined the supportiveness of an environment in terms of 'the relative presence or absence of psychological support resources from significant others'. Similarly, Lin *et al.* (1979) suggested that support was the 'support accessible to an individual through social ties to other individuals'. Essentially, both of these suggestions were simply stating that support is support. Greater focus has been achieved through investigations of the social networks from which support is obtained. The notion 'social network' had emerged from two areas: sociometry and network analysis. Sociometry had grown from Moreno's (1934) investigations of the relationships between individuals within various small groups. He attempted to understand people in terms of the interactions available to them, and various investigators of social support have followed in his footsteps. For example, Berkman and Syme (1979) found that the presence of intimate ties with friends and relatives were strongly related to low mortality rates. Network analysis has very close similarities with sociometry but originated from anthropological interest in interaction among whole communities rather than among small kinship or peer based groups. Social support studies along this line had also observed the importance of social interaction. For example, Berkman and Syme (1979) found that people who lacked community ties had considerably higher death rates than people with extensive social contacts. However, they also found that deficits in family and friendship ties were more strongly related to mortality than were deficits in more general community ties. Implicit in such findings was the idea that intimate types of relationship (such as with friends and family) were the greatest sources of support. This view prompted network theorists to concentrate their investigations on primary groups. The concept 'primary group' was itself quite old and was defined as early as 1909 by Cooley as being characterised by intimate face-to-face interactions. More recently, Broom and Selznick (1973) have defined the primary group as being those people with whom one has both interaction and commitment.[2]

Various investigators (such as Sokolovsky *et al.* 1978, and Hirsch 1980) had noted deficiencies in the quality of primary group contact available at home to psychiatric patients, indicating that it may play a role in their problems. However, it would have been inappropriate to assume on the basis of this that the supports available to an individual could be understood solely in terms of such inter-personal contacts. Investigators, for example, had noted inconsistencies which could not be explained without reference to other factors. For instance, Thomas and Weiner (1974) had found that the relative support provided by different types of network was very dependent on the current needs of the individual. It is obvious, for example, that when involved in some accident, the knowledge that doctors are on their way will provide much more support and relief than the knowledge that a group of friends are rushing to the scene. However, in other crises, such as after a recent death or loss, the company of friends is much more preferable. To understand, therefore, how much support a person was gaining from their current social contacts, it would first be necessary to understand what current crises they were facing, thereby obtaining some idea of their current needs (very much in the same way as described in Chapter 3, when we were discussing how to determine how lonely a person was). This effect of current needs on the benefits provided by a social support will be discussed in greater detail in Chapter 5. However, in the present context, it showed that factors other than network characteristics (i.e. factors other than the people we have contact with) had to be considered. Consistent with this suggestion, Israel (1982) has even pointed out that when considered independently of any additional factors, there is little consistent evidence that network characteristics have any relation to health. In view of this, although network theory could define the major sources of social support, an alternative (more specific) understanding of support *per se* was required.

In an attempt to achieve greater specificity than was possible with traditional network analysis, investigators tried to understand social support by compiling lists of those social experiences within a network which appeared to have psychologically supporting characteristics. Not surprisingly, reviewers have noted several consistencies across these experiences and have tried to organise them into taxonomies of support.[3] For example, Kahn and Antonucci (1980) suggested that the supportiveness of relationships was reflected by three categories of social support. They were affect (the expression of liking, respect, etc.), affirmation (the expression of agreement, etc.), and aid (interactions in which assistance is given – money, advice, etc.). Similarly, Moos and Mitchell (1982) emphasised social companionship, emotional support, cognitive guidance and advice, marital aid and services, and social regulation (which concerns role obligations). Broadhead *et al.* (1983) has reviewed considerable evidence showing that such factors are indeed strongly related to well-being. These taxonomies, however, do not negate the need for network considerations. For instance, as Wellman (1979) has pointed out, network theory provides some idea of which social groups are potential sources for the various supports, making available a useful focus for future research.

Four models of social support

The above taxonomies provide a simple general model of social support (Figure 3).[4] However, the model is incomplete because various studies have shown that, as found above for social networks, social supports actually differ in the types of protection they provide. For example, Thoits (1982) showed that they were not equally effective in providing protection from stress. Similarly, Raphael (1977) found that the supports had a differing effect on speed of recovery from highly emotional operations (such as for breast cancer). Reviewing this literature, Cohen and McKay (1985) suggested that regardless of even abundant general social supports, without appropriate specific support (specific to the

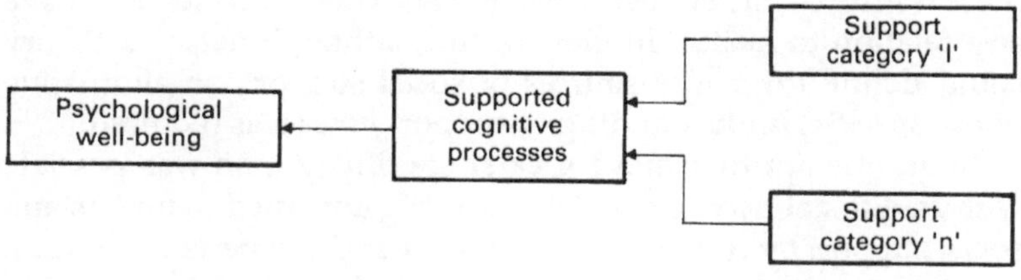

Figure 3 Conceptual framework for exploring social support: Model One.

needs of the individual) well-being would not be protected. Supports, therefore, cannot be treated as being all the same, but should instead be considered separately, thereby acknowledging that each may provide unique benefits to health (Figure 4).

It has also been found that the contribution to well-being provided by a specific support varies according to the circumstances in which it occurs. For example, peer cohesion and encouragement at work is positively related to well-being for men, but not generally for women. Similarly, cohesion and warmth in the family is positively related to well-being for women, but not generally for men (Holahan and Moos 1981).

In a similar vein, the effects of a social support have been found to change depending on who provided it. Advice for example, is perceived to be more helpful when provided by a professional than when offered by a friend (Dunkel-Schetter 1981). Comparable findings have been found concerning the perceived value of other social supports which were provided from different sources (LaRocco *et al.* 1980; Lieberman 1982). These findings clearly indicate that it is not sufficient simply to discriminate between social supports according to their specific characteristics, but also according to the circumstances in which they occur. Accommodation of these issues requires further elaboration to the model below (Figure 5).

Even the above degree of specificity has been described by some investigators as too insensitive to provide a basis for under-

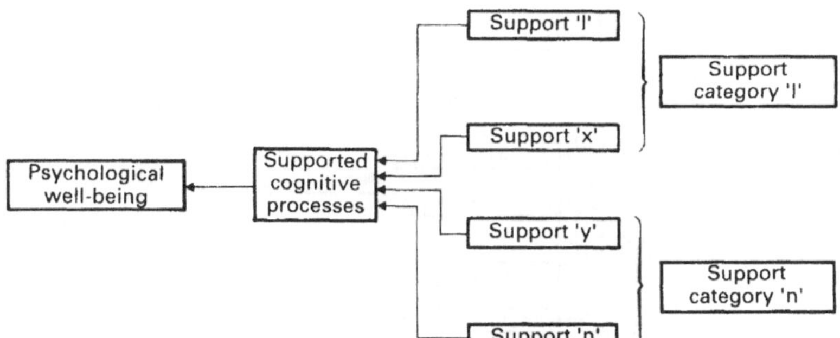

Figure 4 Conceptual framework for exploring social support: Model Two.

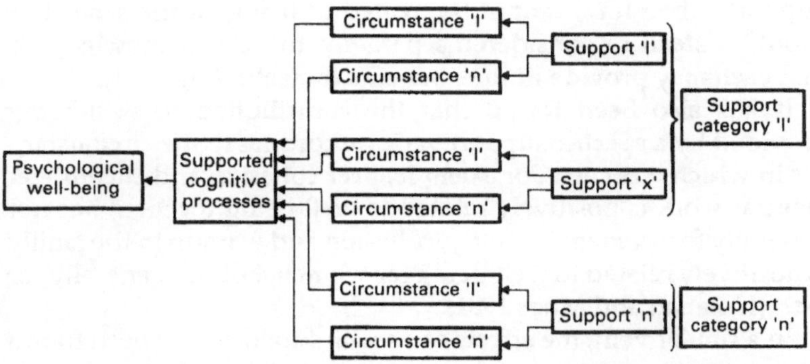

Figure 5 Conceptual framework for exploring social support: Model Three.

standing support. For instance, a further suggestion has been that specific behaviours should be investigated, rather than merely considering the perceived support they provide (Barrera 1981). For instance, when someone provides words of comfort, clearly the way they say it (tone, volume, speed, content), and what they are doing while they say it (embracing lovingly, or watching television), will considerably influence the support which is subsequently gained. These behavioural considerations expand the model below still further (Figure 6).

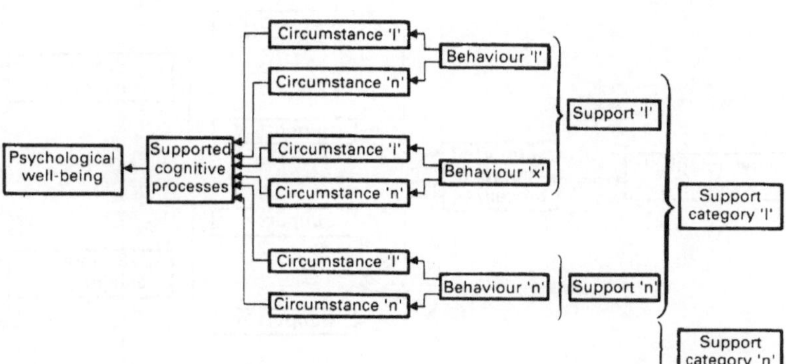

Figure 6 Conceptual framework for exploring social support: Model Four.

SOCIAL SUPPORT VERSUS LONELINESS

Although much of the terminology differs, the above summary of the genesis of the social support paradigm bears a marked resemblance to that of loneliness discussed in Chapters 1 and 2. For example, although beginning with the crude view that social deficiency could be measured simply in terms of number of inter-personal contacts, both now accept that the specific needs of the individual, and the specific behaviours and interactions with which the needs are being met must be considered to accurately evaluate degree of deficit. Furthermore, by comparing the models of social need arising from loneliness theory (Figure 2) and from support theory (Figure 6), overall similarity in strucure can be identified. For example, the specific circumstances and behaviours of the support model compare well with the social resources of the loneliness model. In both cases, what is being referred to are the specific interactions available within a person's social environment. Similarly, the various levels of support indicated in Figure 6 represent the important social experiences needed by people in order to maintain well-being. These compare strongly with the various levels of social need (primary and secondary – Figure 2) arising from loneliness research.

Further contrasting loneliness and social support theory, Rook (1984) pointed out that unlike support deficits, loneliness is characterised by negative emotions such as sadness, anxiety, boredom, self-deprecation, and feelings of marginality. On the basis of this, she suggests that the two notions should be kept distinct. However, the tendency not to find correlations between support deficiency and negative feelings has occurred merely because most social support research has tended not to look for such associations, assuming that being deprived of social supports does not cause negative feelings. However, when investigators have looked into this, the results have been similar to those from loneliness research. For example, people deprived of adequate social supports have been found to be more depressed (Stephens *et al.* 1978) and more anxious (Barrera 1981) than others.

The final issue emphasising the similarity between social support and loneliness concerns the definition of loneliness. Peplau and Perlman (1979) have suggested that feelings of loneliness were synonymous with the perception of any deficiency in the ability of the social environment to provide desired interactions (with greater deficiency promoting greater loneliness). The validity of this definition will be discussed in Chapter 6. However, accepting its validity for the present, then by definition, any lack of social supports in the environment will constitute a deficiency in desired interactions. Consequently, it can be concluded that loneliness is the feeling which arises when there is a deficiency in social supports. The two terms, therefore, are very much related, and in many cases, concern identical personal and social phenomena. Consequently, future chapters will draw heavily on studies of social supports in order to explore adequately the causes and consequences of loneliness.

NOTES

1 A common mistake when referring to social supports is that they mean interactions which are emotionally supportive. However, social supports are any social experiences (enjoyable or unpleasant, emotional or otherwise) which support well-being.

2 To show the kind of social support questionnaires resulting from this perspective, Kessler and McLeod (1984) reviewed those which had concentrated on network characteristics. Details of these questionnaires are given in the appendix, including both 'general network' questionnaires and those concerned with more intimate primary groups.

3 Kessler and McLeod (1984) have reviewed questionnaires that have assessed degree of social support in terms of these specific major supports and/or specific taxonomies of support. Their findings are given in the appendix.

4 This model is not an attempt to illustrate the process by which social support maintains well-being (this will be discussed in chapter 5), but merely to provide a conceptual framework from which to discuss further developments in the investigation of and definition of social support.

Chapter 5

Loneliness and health

Throughout the previous chapter we have referred to the health sustaining qualities of social interaction. There has accumulated over recent years a vast quantity of evidence attesting to this effect, and various theories have been proposed to explain how it occurs. However, there is still much debate on whether the link is strong enough to justify developing treatment programmes to help the lonely. Of course, the simple fact that loneliness is usually an unpleasant experience, justifies the investment of some effort in helping people overcome it. Nevertheless, in deciding priorities, it is important to know whether help is simply reducing discomfort, or having a significant effect on their health.

In the present chapter we will review the various theories and the evidence for a health sustaining role of social behaviour.

WHAT IS THE EVIDENCE THAT LONELINESS CAN INFLUENCE WELL-BEING?

Initially, most of the evidence suggesting that loneliness was related to health had measured (at the same point in time) both loneliness and some aspect of psychological well-being (such as level of depression or anxiety), and determined whether they were positively correlated. Cohen and Syme (1984) have reviewed much of this work, and found mostly positive correlations, which suggested that loneliness and well-being were indeed related in some manner. Unfortunately, this type of study could provide no information about direction of causality between the measured variables. For instance, they could not answer whether it was the loneliness that caused problems of well-being, or whether it was poor well-being that led to feelings of loneliness. To resolve this

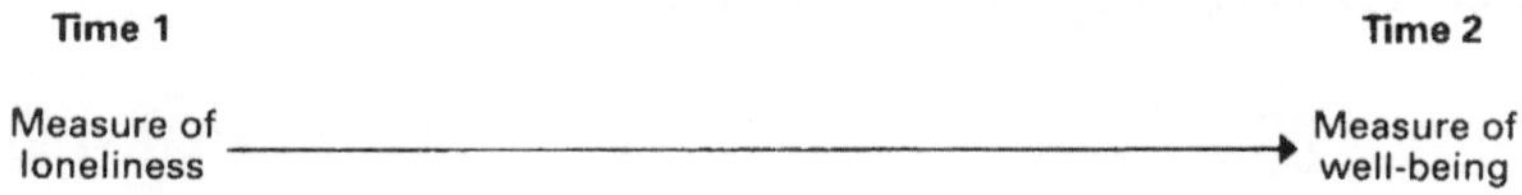

Figure 7 Simple longitudinal design for investigating the effect of loneliness on subsequent well-being.

problem some investigators began to include a time element (or longitudinal component) into their designs. For example, they first measured loneliness and then, at some later time, measured well-being, thereby enabling them to see whether loneliness did indeed lead to changes in well-being (Figure 7). Studies of this type have been much less common than the earlier simple style. Most of those which have been conducted support the idea that loneliness leads to health problems (Broadhead *et al.* 1983). However, several of them produced evidence which undermined this conclusion. Henderson and Moran (1983) for instance, found that social support had no relation to severity of psychological problems. Similarly, Surtees (1984) found that the lack of an intimate partner (a major source of social support – as discussed in Chapter 4) provided no indication of subsequent emotional adjustment. Findings such as these presented investigators with a problem, because on the one hand some studies had found loneliness to be highly predictive of subsequent poor well-being, whereas some, on the other hand, found no relation at all.

Investigators are still trying to clarify whether or not loneliness really does lead to health problems.[1] The overall consensus, however, is that there is indeed a strong link between feelings of loneliness and subsequent psychological and physical well-being. In the second part of this chapter, therefore, we will discuss some of the current ideas about how this link occurs.

MECHANISMS BY WHICH SOCIAL INTERACTION SUSTAINS WELL-BEING

If loneliness does indeed harm well-being, then the goal of the helper is to reduce or reverse this damage, and to protect against further harm. In pursuing this goal, it is important to understand *how* loneliness might undermine well-being. Blindly changing a person's social supports, for example, without consideration of their relevance to health, may do more harm than good. In this context, explanatory theories are few in number, and crudely simple. Nevertheless, they provide some ideas on which social changes will be of most help in dealing with loneliness.

The buffer hypothesis

As was discussed in Chapter 4, research into social support resulted from questions concerning why the prevalence of stressful life events did not cause everyone to be ill. Not surprisingly, therefore, the main theory about how social supports manage to promote well-being revolves around the notion of life events. Cassel (1974), when coining the term social support, suggested that they operated by providing some kind of buffer between people and the stress caused by life events. This has become a popular view, and attempts have been made to explain how this buffering might occur. For instance, at the 1981 conference of the American Psychological Association, Caplan (as reviewed by Broadhead *et al.* 1983) suggested the following six mechanisms.

First, by altering the dimensions of the life event likely to cause the stress. For example, a person's anxiety over a large debt which they cannot pay may be considerably reduced if family members provide financial assistance to reduce the size of the debt. Of course, reducing the size of a stressor need not always involve direct help in this manner. Friends, for instance, may provide that person with (or help them to secure) a job with which to earn more money, or they may teach that person ways of persuading the creditor to extend the payment period.

Secondly, by increasing the accuracy with which the self and the situation is viewed. Remaining, for instance, with the above case of the debtor, anxiety about the debt might lead the debtor to feel that their whole life is falling apart. Friends however, could help the debtor to constrain this growing alarm by encouraging them to focus on more positive aspects of their life. Also, they may help reduce the debtor's feelings of guilt and shame by forcing them to look back and examine realistically both the situation, and the options that were open to them.

Another mechanism proposed by Caplan concerned decreasing the degree to which the situation was viewed as threatening. For example, a well-informed friend may inform our debtor that contrary to their fears, they cannot be imprisoned for late payment of their debt.

A further two mechanisms involved the promoting of neuro-humoral changes which would inhibit or reduce the physiological response to threat. Finally, the sixth mechanism concerned physiological changes which inhibit or reverse the maladaptive consequences of stress.

Many of the above mechanisms have an intuitive validity, and most people will be able to reflect on their own experiences and observe how other people have (in one way or another) helped them in these contexts. Not surprisingly, therefore, considerable evidence has been found for most of the above mechanisms. The bulk of the studies involved, however, have only shown that social interaction influences minor life stresses. Perhaps with most major life problems (which really could have a significant effect on health) this buffering does not occur. For instance, it is commonly found that the presence of other people (family, friends, colleagues) contributes little help to people suffering from the recent death of a spouse. In fact, in cases of morbid grief, the grieving individual can develop severe depression which is resistant to all support from friends and relatives. Clearly, therefore, before acknowledging the buffer hypothesis as a major process by which social interaction protects well-being, extensive further research is needed.

The direct effect hypothesis

Despite the limitations in the buffer hypothesis, it has remained popular. This is partly because a study by Brown and his colleagues (1975) showed that social supports could only be shown to influence well-being if they were considered in conjunction to life events (Model a; Figure 8). However, Tennant and Bebbington (1978) reviewed the data which Brown *et al.* (1975) had used, and found several statistical anomalies. Re-analysing the data, they showed that both life events and social supports could independently exert direct effects on well-being (Model b; Figure 8). This implied that life events were not always involved in the mechanism by which support promoted well-being and that

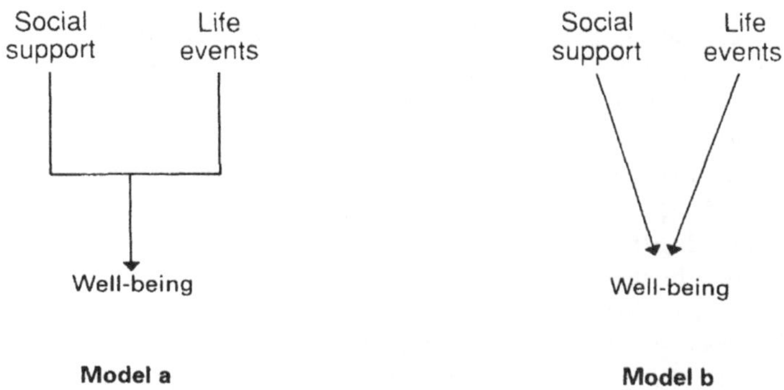

Figure 8 Interactive and direct-effect models of the influence of social support on well-being.

instead support had its own direct effect on well-being. Various mechanisms have been proposed for this. Antonucci and Depner (1982), for example, pointed out how adequate social interaction provided feelings of life satisfaction, which were central to psychological well-being. Consistent with the direct-effect hypothesis investigators have found that even when life events are excluded, well-being is still strongly influenced by social support (Miller and Ingham 1976; Berkman and Syme 1979).

We have seen so far that the effect of at least some social supports on well-being is independent of life events (i.e. has a direct effect, not a buffer effect). Unfortunately, even when a change in support is found to influence well-being, it is often difficult to be sure whether it was a 'buffer' or 'direct' effect. For instance, contrary to the direct-effect hypothesis, perhaps all changes in support constitute a life event and they (like any other life event) have stressful consequences which influence well-being.

Clearly, until investigators can disentangle supports from life events, research cannot really test either the buffer hypothesis or the direct-effect hypothesis. Investigators, therefore, have some way to go before they begin to understand why support seems to promote well-being.

SUMMARY

We have seen above that loneliness has a markedly negative effect on health and general feelings of well-being. This adds considerable importance to help those suffering from severe loneliness. Unfortunately, researchers have yet to clarify how loneliness damages well-being. Consequently, their studies present little with which to guide those who would provide help. We are left, therefore, to depend on checklists and questionnaires with which to delineate where social supports are deficient. Developing such tests is not, however, a simple matter because (as we have seen) people's experiences of loneliness differ, thereby requiring very complicated checklists. The following chapter attempts to overcome this problem, and to present the reader with a basic structure from which to assess loneliness. Subsequent chapters (in Part II) will then give guidelines on how to provide help to the lonely.

NOTE

1 For further comments on the debate, readers are referred to Broadhead *et al.* (1983).

Chapter 6

Measuring loneliness

The unique and varied nature of people's experiences of loneliness presents caregivers and counsellors with a difficult problem of knowing where to begin when a client complains of loneliness. This is particularly important in view of the suggestion in Chapter 5 that loneliness might promote major health hazards. It is necessary, therefore, to have some means of evaluating exactly why, and to what extent, a person feels lonely.

In a similar vein, it is important that further research is conducted to unravel the exact nature of the relation between loneliness and well-being. This, however, also requires detailed assessment of the nature and degree of a person's loneliness. Of course, one obvious method of assessing loneliness would be simply to ask a person how lonely they are. However, this procedure is limited for several reasons. First, people only tend to consider themselves to be lonely once their loneliness has become moderately uncomfortable (as was discussed in Chapter 1), causing many cases of loneliness to be missed by such a method. Another reason is that the assessment would be very vague, making it impossible to draw any conclusions about the type of loneliness they were experiencing (i.e. the type of social resources missing from their lives), which would limit any help that could subsequently be offered. Finally, being lonely is heavily stigmatised in most societies, making it unlikely that people will actually respond truthfully when asked so directly about the quality of their social interactions (Borys and Perlman 1985).

Clearly, therefore, it is necessary to identify a more precise method of assessing how lonely a person is. There are a variety of tests currently to be found in contemporary psychological literature which have been designed specifically to make such assessments. Unfortunately, there are limitations which undermine the usefulness of many of them. The present chapter reviews some of these limitations and provides a new loneliness scale designed to overcome the problems discussed.

In order to discuss the measurement of loneliness it is necessary to have a working definition of the phenomenon. This is because a working definition ties together the various disparate components we have discussed, making it easier to view them collectively. It also ensures that during assessment, disproportionate consideration is not unduly given to any one of them.

A WORKING DEFINITION OF LONELINESS

In order to achieve a definition we must first integrate the three major factors discussed in earlier chapters (e.g. social deficits, norms, and social attributes). We will, therefore, compare and contrast them before discussing potential definitions.

Integrating social deficits, norms, and attributions

Throughout Chapters 2 and 3 much thought has been given to the concept of social deficit, tracing the hierarchical route through which deficits in social resources influence a person's primary social needs. We have also discussed intra- and inter-personal differences in prioritised secondary needs, differing constraints on access to social resources, differences in learned patterns of need, and how each can influence the way a person satisfies their primary needs. However, as discussed in Chapter 1, social deficits constitute only part of the experience of loneliness; social norms and social attributions also have a significant role. We have to a degree paid lip-service to the role of social norms when explaining how norms promote apparent culture differences in social needs. Nevertheless, its significance in the experience of loneliness is much greater than this. To understand its importance more fully, we must return our attention to the hierarchy of social needs and its provision, detailed in Figure 2.

For every social behaviour (or social resource) there are normative expectations concerning its pursuit. Many such expectations are so subtle, or so rarely violated, that they are hardly noticeable. But there are also a considerable number of social behaviours which are surrounded by a great deal of public interest. For example, interest in how much attention is given to a person by the opposite sex, and to how physically aggressive a person is, or how they respond to the aggression of others. Similarly, interest in how attractive a person's spouse is, and in how they behave towards each other; and in how a person's children respond to them and others. This list could go on and on, easily filling the remainder of this book, and for all of these behaviours there are implicit norms dictating what is preferred. Similarly, there are also rules defining how a person should be treated if they deviate from these interaction norms. For example, if a woman is considered to be promiscuous in her relationships, many people will be likely to shun her in compliance with the pressure of public opinion (often through fear that, by association, they might be seen as approving of such behaviours). This would tend not to be the case, however, if the promiscuous person were a man; not because the norms defining promiscuity would be different for him, but because the social rules concerning how one should respond to such a person are different (e.g. many cultures consider promiscuity in a man to be a sign of achievement, and he is treated with approval and envy). In contemporary Western society, many of these values are changing, and it is not the place here to discuss the prejudice behind such sexually discriminating norms. But the example shows that certain interactions have constraining norms, and that deviating from them can have a direct effect on the subsequent availability of other interactions (i.e. because other people may avoid you).

On the basis of these observations we can draw various conclusions about the place of social norms on the hierarchical model defined in Chapter 2 (Figure 2). First, because a person's desire to comply with social norms is promoted by a need to maintain their self-esteem (a primary need), compliance to norms must be a secondary need. Of course, as we have seen in Chapter 1, unlike other secondary needs the effect of norm breaking is mediated by attribution. In other words, breaking a social norm will have most influence on a person's self-esteem if they feel it was the result of their own inadequacies. Such self-blame will arise either because they convince themselves of it (perhaps because it really is their fault), or because other people, by ridiculing or avoiding them, convince them of it. Nevertheless, regardless of this role of attribution in linking self-esteem to deviance from norms, the need to comply can still be considered a secondary need. It is, however, a special type of secondary need, because it can be threatened whenever we interact with other people. Many people, for instance, are continually anxious that they have made themselves look foolish by doing or saying things which are unacceptable. No other secondary need is so widely vulnerable.

Apart from affecting self-esteem, norm breaking also directly affects the availability of social resources. Sometimes the influence may be positive, such as the increased popularity a promiscuous man may find among other males. But, on the whole, it is likely to be negative, leading to a temporary (and sometimes permanent) reduction in the availability of social resources. The effect of social norm breaking will, of course, rarely promote a reduction in all social resources, but will instead tend to influence specific resources with specific people. For example, a child who bullies another may not lose its close friends, but could encounter a reduced level of more general interaction, as other children avoid it. Similarly, a man who gambles away his week's wages may notice little change in the way his peers interact with him, but his wife may refuse to speak to him and ban him from the bedroom. There are, however, some instances of norm breaking (such as incest, or extreme violence) which can lead to complete social excommunication or imprisonment.

The need to comply with social norms, therefore, although essentially being a secondary need, should, by virtue of the extremely wide range of social resources to which it is sensitive, and also the fact that norm breaking can itself influence the availability of resources, be given special consideration when trying to understand loneliness. (The special role of this factor in the hierarchy of needs and their resources has been given in Figure 9.)

Finally, let us consider the label attached to a person when others consider them to be lonely. In Chapter 1 we discussed how the apparently dichotomous nature of loneliness, i.e. that we tend to perceive a person as being either lonely or not lonely, had arisen simply because people were only actually labelled as being lonely once they had reached a critical point on the continuum of loneliness. But how does this label fit into our model of needs and resources? Essentially, it doesn't; not because the model is insensitive, but because the mere label of being lonely does not

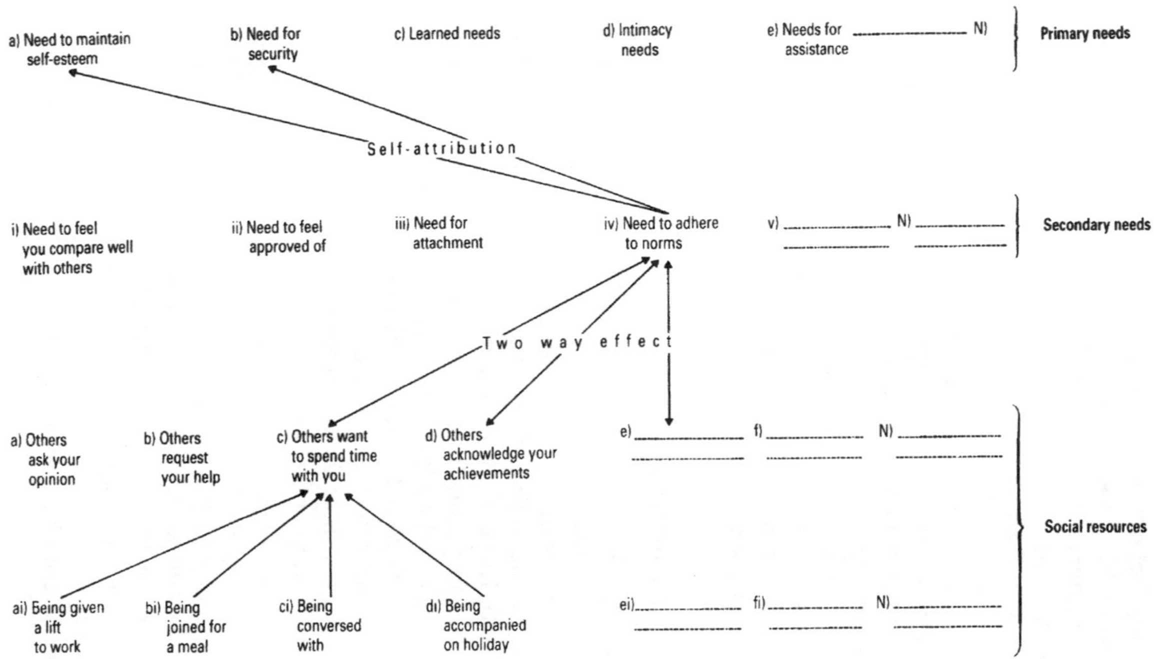

Figure 9 Sample of the hierarchy of social needs and its resources (emphasising the role of the secondary need to adhere to norms).

have a lot to do with the actual experience of loneliness. In this context, it is re-emphasised that loneliness is something that most people experience some of the time; its degree being determined by the extent to which their environment is socially deficient, and to which they feel deviant and odd. The label 'lonely', however, is simply that which is given when the loneliness reaches the point people consider to be unusual. Giving the label in this manner can mislead one into assuming that very few people are in fact unhappy with their social environment, and that everyone else is perfectly content, which is not the case. Consequently, we have not considered it useful or relevant to include this factor in the model of needs and resources given in Figure 2 or Figure 9. Of course, being labelled as lonely effectively implies that a person is not conforming to the norms defining adequate social interaction. It is likely, therefore, to have some effect on their self-esteem. Nevertheless, this is simply another case of undermining the secondary need to comply with social norms, and does not, therefore, justify a special role in our model.

Achieving a definition

Summarising the above, it is possible to achieve an initial definition of loneliness. We can say that loneliness is the feeling a person has when their primary needs are not being met (of course the nature of the feeling will change depending upon which needs are not met). This definition, however, is not very useful because it cannot be operationalised. A definition is considered to be operationalised when it is based on concrete, measurable factors; by virtue of which it dictates the operations by which the phenomenon can be detected and measured. This issue will become clearer if we consider the two main factors which undermine the operationalisation of the above definition.

First, investigators do not currently understand exactly what a person's primary social needs are. We have listed a few in Chapters 2 and 3, but without knowing all of them it is not possible to measure loneliness based on the above definition. There will, of course, come a time when primary social needs are more fully understood, and perhaps then the above definition would become more useful.

As an alternative, perhaps we could look at which social

resources are available to a given person and then simply assume that if they are very limited then his primary needs must be being deprived. This, however, raises the second factor undermining our definition: it is not possible to say which social resources a person will use to satisfy the various primary needs. This uncertainty is caused by the cultural and experiential differences discussed earlier that promote variations in which secondary needs (and therefore which social resources) people use to satisfy their primary needs. Consequently, even the most detailed observation of the social resources to which a person has access to will not reveal which of their primary needs may be being deprived.

In view of these limitations, it is clearly fruitless trying to measure or assess loneliness in terms of the primary needs which may or may not have been satisfied. Consequently, some other basis for our definition must be sought. The problem here is that people differ so much in what is likely to make them feel lonely, that it is very difficult to achieve a single definition which can usefully be applied to them all. Unfortunately, in addition to this, there is a third problem which increases even further the tendency for people to differ: it concerns the way people *perceive* the things they encounter in their social environments. Cobb (1976) has pointed out that many interactions benefit well-being through the information they impart. For instance, interactions which indicated to a person that they were trusted would be unlikely to be beneficial (i.e. satisfy secondary needs such as the need for approval) unless they perceived the implications of the interaction. This significance of perception and mis-perception in deriving benefit from the social resources in our environment has been graphically illustrated in an article which appeared in the *Sunday Times* (1983). The article concerned the experiences of a young widow called Rosemarie Seymour. When Rosemarie's husband died she found that her friends were extremely supportive and helpful. Nevertheless, in spite of their care and concern, she declined to encourage their visits and eventually found herself to be isolated and lonely. Obviously, grief and shock would cause her to avoid people to some degree, but why did she deprive herself so totally of the company and support she clearly needed? Indeed, so great was her need for others that she described 'cowering on the kitchen floor, thinking I had to talk to someone'. Why then did she feel driven to deprive herself of these essential social resources?

The answer lies in Rosemarie's own words. She pointed out that although her friends seemed to be concerned and caring, she believed that it was really her husband they liked, not her, and that they were merely visiting out of respect for him. In reality, it is unlikely that this was the real motive of all of her friends. Nevertheless, the important point here is that it did not matter what her friends actually felt; it was her perception of what they felt (what she believed) that she responded to. This can, of course, happen in the opposite direction to Rosemarie's under-estimation of her friends' intentions. For example, most people will have encountered at some time the unpleasant 'thick-skinned' type of individual whom nobody likes, but they just never seem to realise it.

These mis-perceptions do not only occur during times of crisis, as was the case with Rosemarie, but can be easily precipitated by various common factors. For example, as we discussed in Chapter 2, the degree to which a person mis-attributes responsibility to themselves for things occurring around them is often based on mis-perceptions. Consequently, some people are much more likely than others to blame themselves when a person cancels an appointment or date with them, rather than concluding that something such as illness in the other person caused the cancellation. In fact, some people are so prone to negative self-attribution in this manner, that even if it was explained to them that illness was the cause, they would reject this as a polite excuse believing that the true cause was something they had done.

Another common basis for people mis-perceiving the intentions of others is of course culture. We have already discussed, for example, how Arabs, because of their social distance norms, felt that Americans were being openly rejecting of them; a mistaken assumption which clearly undermined their secondary need for approval. Further errors of perception, also frequent causes of social mis-judgement, are wrongly hearing what a person says, or being mistaken about what you think they did.

In view of the wide range of potential misperceptions, it is clearly inadvisable to establish any working definition of loneliness based on what a person actually encounters in their social environment. This, together with the other problems discussed above, provides a range of selection of criterion with which to constrain any subsequent definition.

1 The definition should not require that the various primary and secondary social needs be listed (as we have discussed, this is currently beyond the scope of social-psychological knowledge).
2 In order to avoid problems concerning intra-and inter-personal differences in patterns of primary and secondary need provision, it must not be necessary to make any assumptions about which social resources are providing for which needs.
3 Consideration must be given to what a person perceives to be occurring in their social environment.
4 The definition must be operationalisable, indicating in concrete terms how loneliness can be assessed.

Fortunately, two researchers (Peplau and Perlman 1979) have produced a concise definition which satisfies each of these criteria. They defined loneliness as the experience which results when a person is not satisfied with their present network of social relationships and feels unable to improve them. This definition provides for the first and second criteria above by operating solely at the social resource level, thereby avoiding the need to make vague connections between resources and needs. It achieves this by including 'satisfaction' as a key factor in the definition. Clearly, if all of a person's primary social needs are being met, then they would be satisfied with the present state of their relationships (i.e. the resources currently available within them). Consequently, a person's degree of satisfaction (or dissatisfaction) will provide a strong *overall* impression of how adequately their primary needs are being met. Of course, it will not be possible to ascertain exactly which primary needs were (and were not) being met, but, as was pointed out above, such specificity is beyond our current understanding of social interaction.

The third criterion has been met, because by asking a person whether they are satisfied with the state of their social resources, one is automatically accessing their subjective world (a person can only be satisfied or dissatisfied with the world as they perceive it). Consequently, a person's reported satisfaction will irrevocably include all of the mis-attributions, cultural misconceptions, and mistaken observations, with which they contort the true nature of their social resources.

Peplau and Perlman's definition meets the final criterion above, because it is possible (as the definition implies) to simply ask a person how satisfied they are with the current state of their relationships. In this manner we have a definition which provides a simple basis for assessing loneliness. Unfortunately, proceeding to measure loneliness on this basis is tantamount to simply asking them how lonely they are, and will consequently fall foul of at least some of the problems discussed at the beginning of this chapter. Therefore, although Peplau and Perlman's definition overcomes the problem of individual differences of perception, it is not a truly working definition. The problem is that in order to be useful, a definition must make some clear specifications about the type of interactions (or social resources) which are deficient. In this context, Peplau and Perlman's definition could be adjusted to refer not to 'present network of relationships' but to satisfaction with a given list of social resources; thereby providing a highly operational definition. In the following section, we will discuss the requirements for such a list.

CLASSIFYING SOCIAL RESOURCES

There are four main issues which must be considered when attempting to identify a list of people's social resources: the type of interaction; the context of the interaction; negative interactions; and intra-personal and inter-personal differences in preferred interactions.

Type and context of interactions

When discussing in Chapter 4 the various models of social support, it was concluded that to reliably assess social deficit it was necessary to consider both the context of interactions and the behaviours involved (Figure 6). Unfortunately, categorising social resources with such a degree of specificity will produce an enormous list of items. Using these to assess loneliness would entail presenting respondents with such a large list of questions that it is unlikely many people would comply. Clearly, therefore, practical constraints limit the specificity which can be included in the list of resources. In view of this, for assessing overall loneliness, it is only practicable to consider general types of resource (e.g. 'others having physical contact with you'; Figure 9) rather than considering specific behaviours (e.g. 'being kissed on mouth'; Figure 9), or specific contexts (e.g. being kissed 'in public, private; clothed, naked; by friend, spouse; opposite sex, same sex').

Negative interactions

Reviewing previous tests, Wortman (1984) pointed out that they emphasised only positive social resources, ignoring experiences which may be undesirable. This omission was significant because some social experiences have a negative effect on well-being (Henderson *et al.* 1978; Fiore *et al.* 1983). For example, being shouted at and abused, being mocked and jeered, or being bullied, can each undermine the need to maintain a positive self-esteem. This is important because it means that loneliness can be promoted not only by a deficit of desirable social resources, but also through over-exposure to undesirable social experiences. Aware of such issues, Henderson and his colleagues (1981) when using their test (the Interview Schedule of Social Interaction – ISSI) asked respondents to indicate both their satisfaction with positive interactions such as being appreciated, and also their dissatisfaction with negative interactions such as arguing. Unfortunately, however, there were limitations with even this sensitive procedure. Inherent in this style of questioning was the unjustified assumption that positive interactions were always positive and negative interactions were always negative. Consider, for example, the negative effect of argument and hostility. Although arguments are often destructive and damaging, Peterson (1983) has suggested that such conflicts could 'lead to a beneficial change in ... the relationship' (p. 381). He pointed out several routes through which this benefit could occur. For instance, the relationship could come to be guided by different rules; understanding could be deepened; and affection could grow stronger. Unfortunately, there is little relevant research evidence with which to test this hypothesis. However, the findings of Fitz and Gerstenzang (1978), Gelles and Straus (1979), and Straus and Hotalling (1980), that it was in the family and heterosexual relationships (some of people's most involved interactions) that most of this hostility was expressed, suggest that the notion deserves serious consideration. This clearly has implications for other social interactions and removes all certainty about how positive or negative their effects are. It is important, therefore, that social resources are compiled in a manner which does not make such assumptions.

Intra-personal and inter-personal differences

As we have discussed in Chapter 3, cultural, sub-cultural, and intra-personal differences exist regarding which social resources a person can make use of. This presents a problem for developing a list of social resources which is relevant to more than one person at a time. Of course, it is a fair argument that we should not try to develop a single common list which ignores people's individuality, but should have a unique list for each person. This may be best when trying to help people overcome their loneliness (although, even here, a general list would provide a useful place to begin), because it means that any subsequent intervention programme would be tailored to suit their individual requirements. However, converting simple lists of social resources into reliable and valid tests is very time consuming (as is described in the Appendix). Consequently, it is useful to have a single test which is flexible and can measure the loneliness on a less individual basis. This raises the question of how one can develop a widely applicable list of social resources which avoids the problems of inter-personal differences we discussed earlier.

One method of minimising the effect of inter-personal differences, is to develop the list from people of a single culture, and to only use it to measure the loneliness of people from that culture. This has tended not to be the case with some tests. For example, the UCLA loneliness scale (developed with Americans) has been used freely with people from various other cultures (see Borys and Perlman's (1985) review of studies using this test). Of course, because of the tendency for variation also to occur across members of the same culture, even taking this precaution will not ensure that the test is completely relevant to all members of the target population. Nevertheless, variation within a culture is likely to be much less than the variation across cultures (where vast differences in social norms frequently exist). It is less important, therefore, that 'within cultural' variation is considered in identifying social resources to be included in a test. Nevertheless, whenever possible, the smaller the sub-group to whom the test relates, the more sensitive subsequent assessments will be.

Despite the fact that it is less important to consider differences occurring within a culture, there are two sub-groups which could not justifiably be ignored. The first concerns people who are emotionally/psychologically disturbed.[1] We have pointed out in earlier chapters that loneliness may have a causal influence on the onset of neuroses. Similarly, some emotional/psychological problems may distort people's need for various social resources. It may be the case, therefore, that a loneliness test developed on the general population would not be relevant for disturbed individuals. It is clearly necessary, therefore, that any serious attempt to develop a list of social resources gives some consideration to psychiatric factors.

The second intra-cultural factor which is too pervasive to be overlooked is that of sex differences. Reisman (1981) has suggested that males and females prefer different types of interaction, with men desiring shared activity and women preferring intimate, confiding interactions.[2] Clearly, therefore, it is necessary when compiling the proposed list of social resources, to investigate the possibility of this sex difference.

A BRITISH LONELINESS TEST

Summarising the present chapter, we have shown that in order to measure loneliness, it is necessary to compile a list of social resources which is relevant to the culture under consideration, avoids assumptions about negativity, and ensures that potential sex and psychiatric status differences are accommodated. One such test, devised for British users, was constructed by Murphy and his colleagues. This is given in Figure 10, and details of its construction and validation are shown in the Appendix.

NOTES

1 Of course it is inappropriate to dichotomise psychiatric disturbance versus non-disturbance in this way, because there are many very different types of psychiatric disorder which are not easily grouped in this manner. Also, in many instances, it is unclear what is really meant by 'disturbed'. Nevertheless, in severe cases of disturbance, mental processes are so distorted that marked differences in social preference may occur. In order to most conveniently accomodate such factors, we will simply categorise disturbed versus non-disturbed.

2 Borys and Perlman (1985) disputed that there was any real difference between the sexes, suggesting instead that it was fear by men about disclosing to investigators their true feelings which had produced this difference effect. However, in earlier chapters we have pointed out major flaws in this latter suggestion, enabling it to be rejected as a criticism of Reisman's ideas. (Nevertheless, it made an important point that there may indeed be fear about admitting to loneliness, and that tests therefore, should avoid this direct type of questioning.)

Figure 10 The MSW loneliness scale

Scoring: Scores for all items indicated (*) are reversed. Average scores for each of the four sections answered are determined. This gives a measure of the supports available in the context of each of the specified relationships. Total scores are determined by evaluating the mean score across these four averages. Low scores indicate social support deficiency.

PLEASE READ THE INSTRUCTIONS AT THE HEAD OF EACH SECTION CAREFULLY YOU WILL ONLY NEED TO ANSWER 4 OF THE 8 SECTIONS

Name:
Age:
Sex: MALE/FEMALE

SECTION A ONLY ANSWER THE QUESTIONS IN THIS SECTION IF YOU *HAVE AN INTIMATE PARTNER* (E.G. BOY/GIRLFRIEND or HUSBAND/WIFE)

		YES	*Maybe yes*	*Maybe no*	*NO*	
1)	Are you satisfied with how honest they think you are?	1	2	3	4	*
2)	Are you unhappy about how confidential they keep things about you?	1	2	3	4	
3)	Are you satisfied with how well they respect your privacy?	1	2	3	4	*
4)	Are you satisfied with the amount of time they like to spend with you?	1	2	3	4	*
5)	Are you unhappy with how they feel if you break promises to them?	1	2	3	4	
6)	Are you unhappy about how well you sexually satisfy them?	1	2	3	4	
7)	Are you satisfied with how honest they are with you?	1	2	3	4	*
8)	Are you satisfied with how well they keep their promises to you?	1	2	3	4	*
9)	Are you satisfied with how well they satisfy you sexually?	1	2	3	4	*
10)	Are you unhappy with the amount of concern they show about your problems	1	2	3	4	
11)	Are you satisfied with how much they appreciate you?	1	2	3	4	*
12)	Are you unhappy about the opinion they have of you?	1	2	3	4	

SECTION B ONLY ANSWER THE QUESTIONS IN THIS SECTION IF YOU *DO NOT HAVE AN INTIMATE PARTNER* (E.G. BOY/GIRLFRIEND or HUSBAND/WIFE)

THE THINGS I MISS ABOUT NOT HAVING AN INTIMATE PARTNER ARE:

		TRUE	*Maybe true*	*Maybe untrue*	*UN-TRUE*
13)	How honest they would think I am	1	2	3	4
14)	How well they would keep my secrets	1	2	3	4

15)	How well they would respect my privacy	1	2	3	4
16)	How much time they would want to spend with me	1	2	3	4
17)	How upset they would be if I broke promises to them	1	2	3	4
18)	How sexually satisfying they would find me	1	2	3	4
19)	How honest they would be with me	1	2	3	4
20)	How well they would keep their promises to me	1	2	3	4
21)	How sexually satisfying they would be	1	2	3	4
22)	How much concern they would show for my problems	1	2	3	4
23)	How loyal they would think I am	1	2	3	4
24)	How much they would appreciate me and the things I do for them	1	2	3	4
25)	How willing they would be to stand by me in times of trouble	1	2	3	4
26)	The opinion they would have of me	1	2	3	4

SECTION C ONLY ANSWER THE QUESTIONS IN THIS SECTION IF YOU *HAVE A CHILD* (NATURAL, ADOPTED, or FOSTERED)

		YES	*Maybe yes*	*Maybe no*	*NO*	
28)	Are you unhappy about how good or bad they are?	1	2	3	4	
29)	Are you unhappy about how often they are ill?	1	2	3	4	
30)	Are you satisfied with the opinion they *think you have* of them?	1	2	3	4	*
31)	Are you unhappy about their honesty with you?	1	2	3	4	
32)	Are you satisfied with how well they respect your right to your views?	1	2	3	4	*
33)	Are you unhappy about how much they expect you to respect their privacy?	1	2	3	4	
34)	Are you unhappy about how much respect they show to you?	1	2	3	4	
35)	Are you unhappy about their mental health?	1	2	3	4	
36)	Are you satisfied with how hurt they are when you have to make harsh comments to them?	1	2	3	4	*
37)	Are you satisfied with how willing they are to stand by you in times of trouble?	1	2	3	4	*
38)	Are you satisfied with how willing they expect you to be?	1	2	3	4	*

SECTION D ONLY ANSWER THE QUESTION IN THIS SECTION IF YOU *DO NOT HAVE ANY CHILDREN* (NATURAL, ADOPTED, or FOSTERED)

		TRUE	*Maybe true*	*Maybe untrue*	*UN-TRUE*	
39)	I often find myself wishing I had a child	1	2	3	4	

SECTION E ONLY ANSWER THE QUESTIONS IN THIS SECTION IF YOU *HAVE A PARENT* (NATURAL, ADOPTIVE, or FOSTER) WHO IS STILL ALIVE

		YES	*Maybe yes*	*Maybe no*	*NO*	
40)	Are you satisfied with the opinion they have of you?	1	2	3	4	*
41)	Are you unhappy about how often they are ill?	1	2	3	4	

SECTION F ONLY ANSWER THE QUESTIONS IN THIS SECTION IF YOU *DO NOT HAVE ANY PARENTS* (NATURAL, ADOPTIVE, or FOSTER) WHO ARE STILL ALIVE

BECAUSE I DO NOT HAVE ANY PARENTS, I SOMETIMES THINK WISHFULLY ABOUT:

		TRUE	*Maybe true*	*Maybe untrue*	*UN-TRUE*
42)	The opinion they would have of me if they were here	1	2	3	4
43)	Their physical health	1	2	3	4

SECTION G ONLY ANSWER THE QUESTIONS IN THIS SECTION IF THERE IS A PERSONS (OR PERSONS) YOU CONSIDER TO BE *YOUR FRIEND*

		YES	*Maybe yes*	*Maybe no*	*NO*	
44)	Are you satisfied with how loyal they are to you?	1	2	3	4	*
45)	Are you unhappy about how honest they are with you?	1	2	3	4	
46)	Are you satisfied with how well they keep their promises to you?	1	2	3	4	*
47)	Are you unhappy about how willing they are to stand by you in times of trouble times of trouble?	1	2	3	4	

SECTION H ONLY ANSWER THE QUESTION IN THIS SECTION IF YOU *DO NOT HAVE ANY FRIENDS*

		TRUE	*Maybe true*	*Maybe untrue*	*UN-TRUE*
48)	I often find myself wishing I had a friend	1	2	3	4

Part II

Practical approaches

Chapter 7

Helping people to overcome loneliness

GENERAL COUNSELLING SKILLS

In Part I of this book we talked at length about the nature of loneliness and its consequences for health and well-being. We have described that although most people experience loneliness to some degree without ill effect, too much can be harmful. Unfortunately, for those that have become chronically lonely the problem is not easy to resolve. Those seeking help for loneliness will probably have tried persistently to deal with it themselves. Their failure is evidence that effort alone is rarely enough. The clichés 'try to meet more people', 'find yourself a boyfriend/ girlfriend', and 'try to get out more', are rarely helpful. For each individual, real help requires careful consideration of their unique experience of loneliness.

When should counsellors suspect that loneliness might be the source of a client's difficulties?

People seeking help through counsellors or similar helpers rarely report that they feel lonely. Instead, they tend to present themselves with the symptoms of loneliness. For instance, they may ask for help with a drink problem, stress, mild depression, or anxiety. They do not include comments about their loneliness because they rarely realise its involvement. The counsellor, therefore, should be mindful that loneliness may not necessarily present itself as a problem directly, but could nevertheless play a significant role in clients' problems.

Feeling lonely does not necessarily mean that a person feels deprived of all relationships. Instead they may feel unhappy about particular aspects of relationships. A person, for instance, may have adequate close friendships, reasonably supportive parents and a loving spouse; yet may still feel unhappy because their spouse spends too much time at work, leaving little time for the relationship. In such circumstances, loneliness may lead to feelings of anger or depression. Family and friends may not suspect that feelings of loneliness are involved and would find this anger or depression rather confusing. Furthermore, the sufferers themselves may not realise that loneliness has an impact on the way they feel, or may feel unable to admit to feeling lonely. In the face of this anger, confusion, ignorance, and denial, the counsellor has a daunting task of supportive exploration.

Clearly a prerequisite in helping someone to overcome loneliness is first to establish whether they are indeed lonely, and then to determine what they are lonely about. This is a difficult task even for those who know the person well. It is a formidable task for the less intimate professional or helper who does not have years of insight into the person's lifestyle and relationships. Consequently, the counsellor must rely on careful discussion to answer the above questions and get a clearer understanding of the situation. The MSW loneliness scale (see Chapter 6) can be of considerable use here. Of course, no checklist can replace personal knowledge of the client; what the MSW scale does, however, is to give a general indication of how the client feels about key relation- ships. The reader is reminded here that the research described in Chapter 6 revealed that lonely feelings arise primarily through problems concerning friendships and close relationships (rather than very casual acquaintances). The MSW loneliness scale does not therefore examine casual acquaintances. However, when trying to overcome loneliness, casual acquaintances provide the client with useful opportunities to practise new skills. The client is less worried about making mistakes in these circumstances, and mistakes that are made will not have negative consequences for these weak relationships.

Having identified how the client feels about key relationships, the counsellor can then establish the following:

1 Is the client feeling dissatisfied about any key relationships that he has?
2 Is the client feeling dissatisfied about any key relationships that he does not have?
3 What elements of the client's relationships seem to be problematical?

On the basis of the above, the counsellor and client need to agree together whether or not loneliness is contributing to their difficulties and make a decision about which aspects to work on together.

Planning a strategy for overcoming loneliness

We discussed in Chapter 2 the various ways in which loneliness has been described (Figure 2).

1 At the simplest level we can describe it in terms of basic behaviours. We can say, for instance, that a person feels lonely because they never feel able to sustain a conversation with others.
2 At a deeper level, we can describe the same person's loneliness in terms of feelings. For example, we could say that they are lonely because failure in conversation makes them feel that people don't like them.
3 At a still deeper level we can describe the loneliness in terms of basic thoughts and beliefs about relationships. Using the same example above, we could describe the person's loneliness as a consequence of thoughts that make them feel worthless.

In each case, we are describing the same person and the same loneliness, but from different perspectives. This has considerable significance for the counsellor. Dealing with loneliness will involve different options depending on which of the three perspectives are chosen by the counsellor. For instance, working at level '1' would involve helping the client with inter-personal skills so as to improve their ability to converse comfortably (see Chapter 8 for details). On the other hand, the counsellor may feel that a problem has deeper roots which may not be reached by focusing on simple behaviours. When subsequently adopting a deeper perspective the counsellor should explore thoroughly which basic needs are being undermined by loneliness (Figure 2). For instance, are the deficits in the client's relationships making them feel inadequate or deprived of social support and companionship, or are these deficits making them imagine that other people think they are odd? Deriving an answer to these questions is not simply a matter of asking the client. People rarely have such a sophisticated understanding of their own experiences. Instead, the counsellor must carefully interview the client to build up a picture of these issues.

Having discovered which basic needs are being undermined, the counsellor can then examine and modify the thought processes involved (basic strategies for achieving this are covered in Chapter 10). Investigating thought processes in order to reduce maladaptive thoughts about relationships can enable the client to feel more confident, thereby allowing further work on inter-personal difficulties. For instance, a common problem when trying to teach people how to improve their inter-personal skills, is that they do not have the confidence to practise these skills. Improving confidence, therefore, facilitates skills training. Similarly, working with a client's maladaptive thoughts can reduce the impact of worries concerning the quality of their social relationships (thereby making them feel less lonely). For instance encouraging a client to confront their belief that poor conversational skills make people dislike them, may stop them avoiding conversation.

The counsellor, therefore, has a range of strategies for dealing with loneliness. Interventions can be made simply by teaching the client compensatory social skills. Or, the counsellor can encourage the client to confront the thoughts that feed loneliness. This can be used either as a primary procedure for managing loneliness, or as an adjunct to a more basic procedure (e.g. by helping to overcome client resistance to practising social skills training). (All of these methods are discussed in greater detail in later chapters.) As a general rule in deciding which methods to use, the counsellor should begin intervention at the most basic level appropriate to the problem (where a minimal intervention will have a noticeable impact on the client's difficulty). Only move to deeper levels of understanding when the first intervention seems blocked or has had little impact.

A framework for helping people change

We have summarised an overall strategy for dealing with the problems of loneliness. What we briefly describe now is the particular counselling environment that allows the counsellor to assess, plan, and motivate the client, and within which the client can begin to understand and learn to cope with difficulties.

The promise of confidentiality is fundamental to counselling. It allows the client to face and work through issues that could not otherwise be disclosed without having to worry about privacy or its effect on others. Sessions should be scheduled for a concrete time; the boundaries of this time kept secure. The counsellor should endeavour to start and finish on time, and allow no interruptions. Choose a setting where there is no likelihood of being overheard and sit near enough to feel in touch, without imposing yourself on your client. Ideally there should be no furniture between you and chairs should be similar in size and comfort so as to avoid making the counsellor seem more powerful or important.

Orienting the client

The way a person behaves in any situation will be dependent on what they expect of that situation. It follows, therefore, that what the client expects from counselling will determine the way they use the experience and consequently what is gained from it. If the counsellor deviates too far from the client's expectations, confidence in the counsellor will be reduced, which will have consequences for compliance with therapeutic procedures. Clients' compliance will also be reduced if the situation has no meaning for them. To avoid this problem, it is important to provide the client with a brief overview of what will take place in counselling. The collaborative nature of counselling should be emphasised; the client should be viewed as a responsible adult capable of solving their own problems with the guidance of the counsellor.

The time-scale of counselling should also be negotiated. In our own practice, clients are offered three initial assessment sessions. After this time we are in a better position to know how many sessions are likely to be required. The nature of the case and motivation of the client makes this quite variable and can range from as little as six sessions to over fifty, but usually problems can be worked through in about sixteen sessions.

Making progress

It is important to make clients aware of the nature of progress in counselling. If their expectations about progress are too optimistic (as shown in Figure 11; presumed progress), then disillusionment

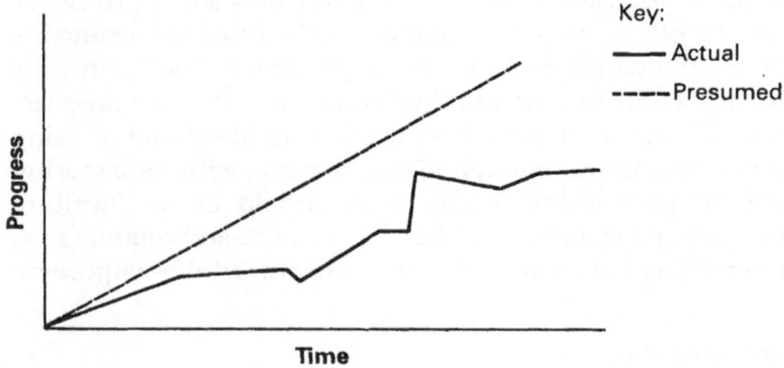

Figure 11 Actual and presumed progress in counselling.

may result at the mere hint of a setback. Counselling is a continual learning process, setbacks should be viewed by client and counsellor as useful information from which to learn. Real progress reflects the amount of 'work' done by the client (including setbacks). This should not end simply when counselling ends; instead skills and techniques learned during counselling need to be to be maintained and improved throughout life.

Motivation

The counsellor needs clearly to understand the client's reasons for wanting to change. If the reasons are weak, based on an impulsive decision to change, or as a consequence of family pressure, then the client's motivation will be minimal. The client needs to be helped to make a strong decision to change. Often clients recognise that their lives will be drastically improved without the problem, but changing behaviours and lifestyles prove more difficult than expected. This needs to be discussed and reviewed, particularly whenever their motivation seems to be flagging. It is also useful to provide feedback on any small gains so that the client can get a picture of how they are progressing.

Increasing awareness

Clients are often confused by their behaviour and will adopt incorrect explanations which can be a source of immense anxiety. Appropriate explanations by the counsellor help the client to demistify their situation. This strengthens the counselling relationship by enhancing the client's positive view of the counsellor and enables the client to make more sense of what is happening to them.

Termination

Although terminating counselling is a natural and desirable goal it is often faced with difficulty by both the client and the counsellor. Ending counselling should be considered and planned either when the client implies that they feel more able to handle things on their own, or when changes related to the objectives of counselling are made.

When terminating counselling its course of progress should be reviewed giving the client credit for what has been accomplished. The client should also be cautioned against believing that the difficulties that they came with are gone for ever. Difficult situations and feelings are likely to be encountered again at some time in the future. The client needs to be prepared to use the skills and techniques learned during counselling whenever, and if ever, difficult situations occur. It should be emphasised that this is not weakness or relapse, but simply a consequence of being human.

Reference to termination should be made well before the last session so that there is time to work through feelings about ending, or about dependency, should this be necessary. The counsellor may decide to space the last remaining sessions at two- or three-weekly intervals in order to make termination a more gradual process. In addition, the counsellor should evaluate the need to follow-up the client after several months, to provide further support if required.

An overview of important counselling skills

Learning to manage loneliness will involve asking clients to open themselves up to new experiences, learn new skills, appraise their thoughts and behaviours, and to look at their difficulties from a different viewpoint. A prerequisite to achieving this is the ability to listen actively, in a warm, empathic, and genuine manner, which serves to reaffirm to the client that they are being understood.

Listening

This is the most frequent activity of the counsellor and requires considerable practice. The more the counsellor understands the client the more effectively the treatment can be planned. The counsellor must be attuned to both 'content' and 'affective' aspects of what the client is saying. This means not simply attending to the verbal component of discourse, but also to the way it is delivered. Components such as speed of response, anger, and anxiety, are all important aspects of any utterance and need to be fully understood.

Paraphrasing and reflecting

Two skills of particular importance in achieving good listening are paraphrasing and reflecting. These show the client that the counsellor is attending, and also enables the counsellor to focus the discussion on to important issues.

Paraphrasing gives a concise translation of what the client has said and reaffirms to the client that they are being listened to (it is aimed at content rather than feeling). Additionally, the counsellor, by providing a 'translation' of the essence of what they think the client has said, establishes a useful check that they understand the client clearly. Summarising and clarifying the client's comments through paraphrasing can also lead to enhanced insight by the client as they begin to think about difficulties from a different perspective.

Reflection is closely tied to paraphrasing, and serves to let the client know that they are being understood. Reflections are often seen as a measure of sensitivity of the clinician. Through them, the client sees the counsellor taking on their frame of reference. They can also be used to encourage the client to disclose further information.

In order to reflect feelings accurately, be sure to attend to both the verbal and non-verbal aspects of the client's communication. Be cautious and tentative in your reflections. This will give room for change if you have misunderstood the client's thoughts or feelings. It is important that the reflection has the right intensity, neither stronger nor weaker than the client is attempting to get across.

Empathy

Empathy involves understanding what the client is feeling, and communicating this understanding sensitively and accurately. Achieving accurate empathy is an extremely complex skill. The key is trying to truly understand (without evaluating) the client's behaviour. Try to understand the reasons the client feels the way they do (perhaps by trying to imagine yourself in their position). Strive not to be judgemental at this point about whether the reasons are unreasonable or illogical; simple understanding without judging is the first step to gaining a meaningful degree of empathy.

Confrontation

Counsellors should be particularly sensitive to the use of confrontation. The general objective here is to challenge the client in such a way as to facilitate progress in counselling. A good counselling relationship needs to be established before one should consider using confrontation.

Questioning

The counsellor should use 'open' questions. These provide the client with an invitation to talk without imposing any structure or frame of reference. An example of an open question is 'how did you feel after that?'. Such questions enable the client to answer freely about what happened. A closed question, on the other hand, such as 'did you feel sad after that?' restricts the client to the counsellor's expectation of events (i.e. that the client should have been sad after the event under discussion).

Silence

Clients use silence in several ways. They may be collecting their thoughts, reliving an experience, or deciding whether or not to disclose a particular point of information. It is important to learn to use these moments without trying to fill them yourself. If you feel the silence has become uncomfortably long, try to intervene without losing what the client may have been feeling at the time (e.g. 'what were you thinking about just then?').

SUMMARY

1 Be aware that loneliness may contribute significantly to a client's difficulties without their necessarily disclosing it (or even being aware of it).

2 Gather information on the adequacy of the client's social relationships and clarify those aspects of their social environment with which they feel dissatisfied. Remember the following skills:

(a) Open questions
Can you tell me a little more, what/when/where/how?
(b) Summarising
Let me see if I've understood this, What you're saying is . . .
The main issues we've discussed so far are . . .
(c) Probing
Lets go through that again in detail.
Give me an example . . .
What happened after that?
(d) Stimulating client based suggestions
How would other people approach this?
How else could you get around that?
What would your next step be?
(e) Paraphrasing
So what you're saying is . . . [content] . . . which left you upset/ angry etc [feeling].
(f) Reflecting
It sounds as if . . . was a difficult experience for you.
(g) Confronting
On the one hand you have said that you will do XYZ, but you have also said that you will do ABC; how will you manage both?

3 Remember that loneliness can be viewed from several perspectives and at various levels of sophistication. Focus on the perspective that will both:

(a) Have most impact on the client's problems;
(b) Require minimal intrusion into the life and thoughts of the client (i.e. work at a simple educational/skills training level where possible, and only proceed to thought management when other options fail). NB *Thought management type interventions should only be attempted under qualified supervision.*

Detailed advice on educational/skills training, and on thought management type interventions, are given in the following chapters.

Chapter 8

Teaching new social rules

Many problems with social relationships occur as a result of poor knowledge of the basic rules of social interaction. An important role for the counsellor involves teaching these rules to clients. In order to focus this teaching, it is important to assess what the client is deprived of in their social relationships. This can be difficult, because:

1 the client seems only able to express their feelings in terms of their primary needs (e.g. 'I do not feel confident with people') and resists further help until the need is resolved (e.g. 'I will be able to mix better when I feel more confident');
2 the client latches on to one relationship as a panacea for all his lonely feelings (e.g. 'I wish I had a girlfriend') and is reluctant to accept that any other changes (such as simply 'getting on' better with people) will help.

In the former example, it is important for the counsellor to help the client to see that the primary need (e.g. to feel more confident) will only be satisfied if they first meet more of their secondary needs (e.g. to be able to sustain some form of interaction with others – Figure 2). This of course, requires that the counsellor learns which aspects of social interaction are a problem for the client (e.g. forming relationships, deepening relationships, or simply the ability to 'chat' with people). Similarly, with the latter example, the counsellor needs to learn what is really missing in the client's social relationships, so that the counsellor may direct them to more suitable methods of resolving their loneliness. Of course, in some cases finding a girl or boyfriend will help the client to feel less lonely. More typically, however, many types of social relationship must be examined in order to deal effectively with their problem.

Having drawn some conclusions about what seems to be missing in the client's social relationships, the counsellor may then decide that training in basic rules and skills of interaction may help. The remainder of this chapter outlines some of the more common areas where instruction is required.

UNDERSTANDING THE RULES OF INTER-PERSONAL BEHAVIOUR

Before one can behave appropriately in a given social situation one has to be aware of the rules that govern particular situations. Clients need to discriminate appropriate from non-appropriate behaviour and to be knowledgeable and consistently aware of the signals and nuances that cue particular behaviours. These cues are based on both verbal and non-verbal communication channels. The latter non-verbal type of communication is an area where difficulty is commonly encountered.

Everything we do tells others something about us. Even when we prefer to hide what we feel, we can be prevented from this by 'leakage' through our behaviours. For example:

Intent: trying to hide anxiety.
Non-verbal leakage: tapping foot; drumming fingers; clenching fists.

Non-verbal behaviours can be useful, often adding impact to our speech or helping us to express ourselves more clearly. Unfortunately, we also exhibit them without realising it, and consequently (through these behaviours) we risk inferring things that we do not intend. Consider, for instance, your last verbal interaction and go through the checklist below see how much you 'gave away'.

1 How close were you in physical distance to the person you were speaking to?
2 What gestures accompanied your speech?
3 How loud were you speaking?
4 How quickly were you speaking?
5 How much eye contact did you have?
6 What was your facial expression like?

Subtle changes in any of these factors can markedly influence what people think we are saying to them. It is unfortunate, therefore, that we are never given formal tuition on how to control our non-verbal behaviour. How close we stand to people, how much eye contact to use, and what gestures we use, are all important communications. However, clients with interactional difficulties often learn some of these aspects inappropriately. This means that they are not only at risk of upsetting and irritating people that they try to get to know, but they also can decode other people's signals inappropriately, leading to confusion about where interactions and relationships are going.

It is important to make clients aware of the norms of interaction before teaching the appropriate skills. The following will help counsellors to do this successfully.

UNDERSTANDING NON-VERBAL BEHAVIOURS

A comprehensive account of non-verbal behaviours is beyond the scope of this book. We will focus therefore on those non-verbal behaviours which are particularly important for social interaction.

Personal space

Our awareness of personal space and the distances at which we feel most comfortable with others are related in some ways to a primitive territorial instinct. We tend to view the immediate proximity as our own and feel uncomfortable if this is intruded upon. However this is very dependent on people and settings. In general, the better we get to know someone the smaller the distance between us (Argyle 1969). The more intimate we become socially and emotionally, the more intimate we get spatially. This is usually reciprocal, with both parties feeling more comfortable at closer distances. Personal space can be differentiated into distinct zones:

Intimate – Zero (i.e. direct contact) to about 18 in (46cm)

> This zone is entered by a close relative or friend, someone making a sexual advance, or somebody hostile who is threatening an attack.

Personal – 18 in (46cm) to about 4 ft (1.4m)

> This zone is entered by casual friends and acquaintances (e.g. the distance we keep from others at social gatherings).

Social – 4 ft (122cm) or more

> We tend to keep this distance for strangers or people we do not know very well (business and impersonal encounters).

We are comfortable (to a degree) with strangers moving within our social and personal zones. However, intrusion into the intimate zone causes discomfort. This means that touching someone you have just met may result in that person feeling negative towards you (though they may hide their annoyance in order not to cause offence).

The reason that we sometimes perceive a new work setting as 'cold' or 'unfriendly' can also be related to proximity. New colleagues keep their social distance appropriately at the social zone until they know us better. As time passes we enter more intimate social zones and feel warmer towards our colleagues.

It is important for clients in counselling to be aware of these issues, particularly when meeting people for the first time. Only when a relationship becomes more intimate, can the physical distance become closer.

Eye contact

The length of time people look at us or hold our gaze as they speak often has consequences for how comfortable we feel with them. Gaze can be an indicator of intense liking. As well as direct gaze, the pupils provide further information. Mood changes, for instance, can be interpreted through pupil dilation or contraction. When a person becomes aroused or excited their pupils can dilate to up to four times their normal size. Conversely, anger can cause them to contract noticeably.

The amount of eye contact during interactions provides further data. Sparse eye contact can indicate deceit; intense eye contact, on the other hand, can mean two things:

1 the person finds you attractive (which will be associated with dilated pupils);
2 the person is angry or issuing you with a non-verbal challenge (in which case the pupils will be constricted).

Clients need to be made aware that to develop good rapport they should attempt to meet the gaze of the person they're talking to about 60 per cent of the time. Some clients, however, find direct eye contact difficult. In these cases it is worth suggesting that they aim their gaze at the centre of the forehead of the person that they are talking to. They will find this easier, and, to the other person, it feels like direct eye contact.

DEVELOPING INTER-PERSONAL SKILLS

Interpersonal difficulties are not easily dealt with by fixed procedures or techniques. Clients require an approach that is flexible enough to accommodate alternatives as situations change. The framework for inter-personal skills training preferred by the present authors is based on a problem solving approach. Initial work in this area by D'Zurilla and Goldfried (1971) suggested that a person's ability to cope with inter-personal situations is based on an ability to use problem solving skills. Clients are first introduced to the general approach to problem solving before being taught specific skills. Interpersonal problem solving involves the following stages:

1 identification and definition of the problem situations;
2 breaking the problem into manageable pieces;
3 gathering information about aspects of the situation;
4 generating a broad range of possible solutions;
5 dismissing solutions which are least feasible;
6 trying out the most feasible solutions;
7 evaluating outcome;
8 if necessary, redefining, revising, and retrying again.

The client and counsellor should initially work together to formulate and work through the problem based on the stages listed above. In time, the counsellor should urge clients to follow this framework themselves every time they encounter a difficult situation.

TEACHING INTER-PERSONAL SKILLS

The client should first be provided with didactic information concerning appropriate social behaviour. This can be accomplished verbally within the session, but should be backed up with short handouts for the client to read and take away.

The counsellor should then choose a skill to be developed which is:

1 the least complex (among the skills in which the client is deficient);
2 predicted to have the greatest probability of success.

This will allow the client to feel that progress is being made and will increase motivation to learn further, more complex skills.

By this point the client should understand the goal of the new skill and the way that it fits into social interactions. In progressing on to improve the skill, we cannot simply tell the client how to behave. We need to use all the channels of communication available to us. This is best accomplished through modelling and role-play where the counsellor demonstrates relevant skills to the client. Modelling of performance can take two forms. In the first (offered by Meichenbaum 1977), the counsellor acts out the skill and allows the client to watch them make errors initially, and then recover from them. Alternatively, a 'sliding' model can be incorporated. This involves modelling simple skills appropriately but erring occasionally on the more complex ones. With both methods, the client sees that failure is not disastrous, and that it can be overcome.

The next stage of modelling involves the client rehearsing (or role-playing) the specific skills required with the counsellor. This should also include cognitive rehearsal of what the client thinks, expects, and tells himself about the forthcoming scenario. The first attempt at practising the skill is usually anxiety provoking, so clients need to be warned of this. It is useful to use early sessions simply to feedback the strengths and weaknesses of the client's present functioning before adding the stressor of learning a new skill. In later sessions the client may practise the skill in a safe setting.

After the role-play is over, feedback is offered either through observer notes or video record. The function of feedback is to provide information which both motivates the client toward further improvement and provides guidance for specific change. This means looking for strengths wherever possible and couching weaknesses in terms of approximations to the initial model behaviour. Saying, for example, 'you have not used as many gestures as I did', rather than 'you are still not using any gestures'.

Homework assignments and maintaining gains

After a target skill has been performed satisfactorily in the session it should then be tried out in real life through the use of homework assignments. These expose the client in a graded fashion to difficult situations and emphasise the client's responsibility in working through their difficulties. They also emphasise to the client that change occurs between (rather than within sessions) and is dependent on their efforts. In addition, homework provides useful data on how well skills are being taken on as well as the client's work rate and motivation to proceed.

Homework also serves as a useful first step towards helping the skills learned to generalise to the client's natural environment. Generalisation is not a passive phenomenon but needs to be planned actively. This involves the client and counsellor collaborating to establish where and how the client can practise newly acquired skills. For initial attempts, the client should practise on casual acquaintances (weak ties). These are favoured because of the following characteristics:

1 there are no strong emotional attachments;
2 there are well-defined role definitions which reduce uncertainty;
3 exchanges are usually simple and instrumental, and making mistakes here will have relatively little consequence for the client.

Because weak ties are detached from the client's social circle they can practice new behaviours and try out new identities which would be too threatening to attempt with stronger relationships.

The client's experience of inter-personal effectiveness through role-play and homework serves to promote use of newly learned skills throughout their social environment.

First encounters – an inter-personal skills compendium

First encounters in relationships are extremely important. They not only set the scene and agenda of the present encounter, but also lay the foundation for future interactions. Some tuition in this area will be useful to many clients. There are three distinct phases to teach.

Opening the interaction

Conversations are generally opened with a non-verbal signal. Clients often focus wholly on themselves, thereby missing and being unaware of these 'invitations' to interact. These include:

gestures;
smiles;
nod of head;
making room (i.e. making space in group);
direct eye contact.

The client's agenda for the first few minutes in a social setting should be to try and defocus from self and to attempt to focus on and analyse the non-verbal communication of the people in the room. The goal here is to be mindful of the particular signs listed above, and reciprocate them if appropriate.

Following the initial greeting ice-breaking techniques should be used. These are utterances which have little to do with the main goal of the interaction. They are generally statements about the weather, topical events, or current affairs which are not too controversial.

A useful way of beginning a conversation is to ask an open question which will require more than a simple response (closed questions can usually be answered with a single word). For instance:

Closed question
Person A: Enjoying the party?
Person B: Yes.

Open question
Person A: How do you know the Robinsons?
Person B: Well, Jim's my oldest friend . . .

Maintaining the interaction

After starting a conversation, some clients run into difficulties for two reasons. Some feel they have nothing to say after the initial pleasantries; others, having started conversing, just don't know when to stop. Clients need to be made aware of the particular signals for maintaining conversations. Signals that the listener wants conversation to continue can include:

asking questions;
supplementing the story;
staying close to the speaker;
head/body lean forward towards the speaker;
good eye contact maintained.

If these signals are present the client can then try out specific techniques to maintain the conversation. These involve the use of *probes* to encourage people to expand on their initial utterance. There are several different types of probe which can be used in a number of ways.

Extension probes

'That's interesting, tell me more.'
'And then what happened.'

Echo probes

These echo some of the words of the respondent. They are effective but should not be overused.

A: 'Then I told him I would find another car dealer.'
B: 'Find another car dealer?'
A: 'Yes, I said if that was the way they did business . . . '

Non-verbal probes

When a person finishes talking, sometimes a simple nod or smile is sufficient to indicate that you are interested and want them to say more.

Closing

Closing an interaction is simply drawing attention to the end of a satisfactory conversation and is usually accomplished in a rather ritualistic fashion. Signals that clients should look for as an cue to close the conversation include:

erratic eye contact – glances round room, at watch;
disjointed observations;
conversation kept short.

Clients should be urged to make the first steps toward closing themselves. This gives a feeling of control, and also adds a certain structure to the conversation. Simple statements like, 'well, I must be going now' or 'is that the time?' are good first steps in closing.

SUMMARY

1 Clients need to be taught social rules as a framework for learning new skills.

2 Non-verbal communication can add impact to speech but can also unsettle interactions. Teach clients to use appropriately various aspects of non-verbal behaviour.

3 Learning inter-personal skills is a dynamic process which follows a problem solving approach. Clients need to understand the basics of problem solving before being taught specific skills.

4 Identify a skill to begin teaching which is not too complex and has a good probability of success. Success will motivate the client to work further on more complex skills.

5 Actively plan to help the skill generalise to the client's natural environment with well-thought-out homework assignments incorporating 'weak ties'.

Chapter 9

Maintaining and deepening relationships

As has become evident in previous chapters, developing a relationship is not simply a matter of turning on the appropriate non-verbal behaviours, throwing in a few attitudes and beliefs, and waiting for the friendship to deepen. We have discussed earlier the basic skills required to begin a social relationship. However, if a person is successfully to develop some of these relationships into deeper friendships and partnerships, they must be familiar with the strategies of slowly demonstrating to others that they like them.

DEEPENING RELATIONSHIPS

Without the skill of showing liking to others, it is almost impossible to move from casual acquaintance to greater closeness. For instance, if a man suddenly tells a woman that he has just met that he 'really fancies her', he risks offending her and loses any chance of building a relationship. If however he 'chats' generally about things which seem to interest her he begins to establish the foundations for 'mutual liking', the core of close relationships. This is valid across all relationships, even across the same sex, people are wary of each other at first, and only with time and caution are they willing to admit affection openly.

If social rules prevent us from telling people that we like them directly, we need to develop more subtle ways of communicating this, particularly at the beginning of relationships. Bell and Daly (1984) have identified behaviours and strategies used by people to both appear likeable and let others know they are liked. These include:

being rewarding and enjoyable to be with;
appearing dynamic, interesting and attractive;

taking charge of conversations, while still encouraging others to talk;
appearing open and trustworthy;
skillful use of social manners and rules;
being sensitive and supporting;
being a careful listener;
integrating others into your activities;
pointing out similarities between other and self.

Being liked by others involves two factors. The first is a knowledge of the behaviours which enable us to be seen in a positive fashion by the person we are intent on developing a relationship with (behaviours such as those listed above). The second is the ability to communicate that behaviour. To enable the client to achieve this, it is useful to provide them with a strategy to simplify the task. The following will help here. Consider, for example, striving to appear rewarding and enjoyable to be with (item one from the list above):

Step 1 – Gather information

We first need to identify the subgoals that make up the overall goal. These can usually be broken down into specific behaviours, e.g.:

What would the other person find enjoyable?
What are their likes?
What are their dislikes?
What are their favourite topics of conversation?

Examples of information gathered may include:

Enjoys watching wildlife programmes on television;
Hates people talking when the news is on television;
Enjoys country walks;
Is interested in alternative medicine;
Is interested in the environment;
Likes simply being together without necessarily having to chat.

Step 2 Choose items from the list that are mutually rewarding

Step 3 Follow through

Actively make time to engage in the above while together.

Each of the above steps can be viewed as a goal to be attained, broken down into important subgoals, and then implemented within relevant relationships.

Central to the process of deepening relationships is a gradual learning about the other, and allowing them slowly to learn about us. As we saw in Chapter 2, this process can be likened to penetrating slowly through the layers of an onion. First we learn about superficial aspects, then slightly deeper issues and so on. The depth of penetration or closeness depends on a range of factors. We prefer to keep some relationships superficial and so limit how deep we enter into each other's lives. More importantly the level of penetration that we allow a person to achieve depends on how much we like them, how much they allow us to learn about them, and how much we trust them with our hopes, dreams, uncertainties, and anxieties.

We feel wary about those who disclose too much about themselves or clumsily try to barge in on our personal lives. The key factor here is tentative caution both in striving to learn about others and in permitting them to learn about us.

It is difficult for a counsellor to know how healthy a client's relationships are, or how well they are progressing, without resorting to 'gut feelings'. This is because people vary so much in what they require from relationships. The following list can be a useful guide and can provide people with a more objective indicator of the strength and adequacy of their close relationships. Closeness is often a reflection of the extent to which:

Praise and criticism can be expressed between members;
each member's wants and needs are recognised and met;
pastimes and activities are enjoyed together;
hopes and goals are linked together;
support and nurturance is given without resentful feelings of obligation;
friends, family, and acquaintances are known and shared.

MAINTAINING RELATIONSHIPS

In previous sections we have focused on the indicators and goals that clients need to aim for in building relationships. There comes a point where both parties become satisfied with the state of the relationship, where the level of 'closeness' is acceptable to both parties, and where the relationship begins to run on automatic pilot. We all have ideas about what we see as an ideal relationship, with the ideal person being highly supportive, friendly, nurturing, and stimulating. Most people do not really expect to meet such ideal companions, but some people make themselves lonely by believing that they cannot be happy without finding this ideal person. It is important for the counsellor to help the client to understand that difficulties, arguments, and conflicts, are a normal part of relationship development. In fact, such conflicts should (to a degree) be viewed as opportunities to build and develop the relationship. Conflicts tend only to become damaging to the relationship when they are used to reciprocate hurt rather than to communicate effectively and to work through difficulties.

Maintaining relationships involves knowing how to deal with difficulties as they arise. This involves recognising them early, understanding the phases of possible relationship breakdown, and having options to explore and remedy the difficulties together through effective communication and joint problem solving. A useful framework for exploring these issues was presented by Duck (1982).

Recognising difficulties

The first phase of a possible relationship breakdown involves a realisation by one member that the relationship is in difficulty. Often, the problem is not communicated to the partner at this stage, but may be shared with relatively anonymous others. Although useful, this can lead to a feeling that 'everyone understands except my partner', which can serve to maintain and exacerbate the client's problem. The earlier both partners realise that there is a problem, and the sooner a decision is made to confront the difficulty, the more likely it is to be resolved. There is no chance of resolution if the problem is not communicated.

Often relationships can end before any open acknowledgement (between partners) that a problem exists. This can be because they feel that talking could be too painful, or that the problem is simply too difficult to resolve. Interventions at this phase rely on one partner making the difficulty overt. This is not simply the job of the partner who has identified the difficulty; both partners need to be able to recognise the early warning signs of trouble. These are many and varied and are best recognised through bouts of uncharacteristic behaviour which may include:

undue tiredness;
angry outbursts;
reduced eye contact;
prolonged silences.

Confronting difficulties

Having recognised that there are problems, it is important for members in the relationship to make a decision to do something about it. Success here requires that members learn the skills of recognising hurtful and inefficient communication, and learn how to communicate effectively, and solve problems as they arise. There are three factors to consider here.

Increasing specificity in communication

One of the main reasons why difficulties aren't resolved is because they are often discussed in rather vague, global terms like:

'You don't care about me the way you used to.'
'You've changed.'
'I can't seem to do anything right.'
'We fight all the time.'
'You don't love me.'

These terms have an entirely subjective frame of reference. They label the problem in terms of feelings. This is often a necessary first step towards change, but to begin the process of change and improvement of the relationship, discussions about difficulties need to become *behaviourally specific*. This involves teaching the client to go through the following process.

1 Pinpoint what was felt at the time you are about to describe.
2 Specify how your partner's behaviour was related to this feeling.
3 Specify the situations where the above occurs.

Gottman *et al.* (1976) describe this process as the XYZ formula (I feel X when you do Y in situation Z, e.g. I feel upset (X), when you make fun of me (Y) in front of our friends (Z)). This communicates the difficulty clearly, thus providing specific information about the problem to be worked on.

Achieving accurate information exchange

In addition to improving specificity, we need to make sure that clients receive and work on accurate information. This is best accomplished through teaching them paraphrasing skills, so that they can rephrase what has been said (with their partner) in a tentative fashion to check the accuracy. For instance, 'It sounds like you're saying . . ., have I got that right?'; similarly, 'When you said . . ., was that what you meant?'.

Identifying faulty aspects of communication

As part of the process of learning to increase accuracy of communication, the client must learn to identify faulty aspects of communication. The following list highlights the type of conversation errors that lead to the feeling that 'talking makes things worse'. The errors can be split into two distinct types.

The first type of error involves verbal attacking. The impetus here is to ventilate ones own thoughts and feelings with little concern for resolving the situation. It occurs in several ways.

1 *Self-summarising*. Here, each member's goal is to get their point across without attending to the concerns of the other.

2 *Sidetracking*. This involves continually defocusing from the issue at hand and bringing in other concerns without really trying to work on the issue at hand. This leads to a move away from the issue as well as adding more fire to the problem.

Person A: Why are you so late?
Person B: I'm sorry, I had so much work to do.

Person A: Typical! Your father was just the same, never at home.
Person B: That's not fair, he never . . .

Person A: Your life is just as chaotic as his was.

Person B: How can you say that, when I have to organise everything for you?
Person A: So what if you organise things for me occasionally, what else do you do around the house?

The point here is that the original problem about arriving home late has become 'sidetracked' to issues about family, organisation, and domestic affairs.

3 *Kitchen sinking*: This error involves throwing in almost every difficulty that has ever evolved in the relationship in an attempt to win an argument. The underlying issue here seems to be 'you're at fault here just as you were at fault in situations a, b, c, etc.'

Person A: Are you going to be working again this weekend?
Person B: Maybe, only Saturday.
Person A: I don't know what is wrong with you. I hardly get to see you. The week after we were married you started opting out. I've had to bring up the kids. You hardly know they exist. You couldn't even make the school open evening last year.
Person B: The open day!
Person A: The same reason you never have time for me either. Mother always said I was too good for you. She could see straight through you from the first day she met you....

Both partners feel unable to get their point across and feel hurt and not listened to. The difficulty becomes so vague that there is no starting point for dealing with it. Conversations end without resolutions, and issues that were only partly resolved are brought up again and used as further ammunition.

The second type of error involves thoughts, beliefs, and actions, that can trigger verbal fencing.

1 *Mind reading*: People often believe that they know friends' or partner's thoughts or feelings about particular events, and that they can anticipate their behaviour in certain situations. This can lead to anticipating and reacting to issues before one has sufficient information, or to reacting to an imagined event that may never happen. When we behave like this, we are seldom dealing with the facts.

2 *Third party involvement*: There is often a need to bring in others to backup individual's points of view. This needs to be strongly resisted as it simply adds to the problem.

3 *Hidden agendas*: Sometimes certain behaviours which are often quite innocent in themselves serve as a trigger for emotion and argument between partners. The behaviour often takes on an entirely different meaning for one of the people in the relationship. For example: Partner A (Stephen) does something to upset or annoy Partner B (Freda). Freda asks Stephen to stop the annoying behaviour.

At this point, we have simply described the overt interaction (i.e. the behavioural situation). However, the difficulty with hidden agendas is that they revolve around or are linked to feelings which are often unknown to the first party, such as: Freda feels that if Stephen loved her, he would stop the annoying behaviour.

If Stephen does not stop the 'annoying' behaviour Freda's resulting distress could be out of proportion to the minor annoyance caused by his behaviour. In addition, Stephen is unlikely to understand why a simple behaviour is causing so much upset.

What we are left with here is a behaviour which has taken on new meaning and importance for one member, but is still seen as a relatively meaningless behaviour by the other member of the dyad.

Clearly, it is essential to ensure that the hidden agendas do not go unnoticed in counselling simply by attending to the problem behaviour. The counsellor must attend both to the explicit behaviour, and to any hidden agendas.

Joint problem solving

Mutual problem solving follows a negotiation framework and is a useful adjunct to developing communication skills. The techniques below are based on the strategies discussed in the previous chapters, but they have been adapted so as to be specific to dyads.

Step 1: Identifying and working towards a mutual understanding of the problem

This requires the skills of active listening and specifying one problem at a time. The first negotiation involves identifying a mutually acceptable time. Attempting to discuss important issues while the partner is watching a favourite TV programme, or when they are about to leave for work, is unlikely to be fruitful. Partners need to find a setting that facilitates frank discussion of the issues at hand.

Step 2: Working towards a compromised solution

To become successful problem solvers clients need to learn to treat their partner's *feelings* as if they were *facts*. These feelings may be surprising and highly incongruent with the way they themselves feel about the relationship. Nevertheless, they should not confront these feelings as false or silly. To do so will often lead to fruitless time arguing about whether or not the other's feelings are correct. These may generate feelings that talking is pointless. Instead, it should be recommended to clients that they treat their partner's feelings as if they were correct and move toward discussing the actions that lead to the feelings.

Step 3: Cost benefit analyses of solutions

The final step involves brainstorming for a wide range of potential solutions. Couples should not judge any of the solutions at this stage but simply focus on listing several possibilities.

Solutions to any problem between two people will involve negotiation and can be categorised in terms of their outcomes.

1 *Win–Lose*. This outcome results in one person taking home all the prizes. They dominate the other person and focus only on winning.

2 *Lose–Lose*. This results from one person not being able to stand the thought of the other winning so they make sure that the other person loses even if this means sabotaging their own successful outcome.

3 *Win–Win*. This requires the willingness of both parties to compromise in order that each can win something. They cannot

get to 'win–win' without striving to understand each others wants/needs, clarifying and verbalising their own, and acknowledging the need to compromise. If the goal of any argument is winning unconditionally, the relationship loses.

Participants need to work together to estimate how much effort needs to be expended in implementing the various solutions and which solution will have the largest impact on the relationship. It will also require an input of effort that both parties see as being reasonable. It is often useful as a first step to try to work on a solution that has the most chance of being successful with minimal effort. This will provide motivation both to continue with the approach, and to employ it for forthcoming problems.

Any solution will need effort, testing, refinement, and possibly renegotiation. The solution will need to be given a fair chance, and both client and counsellor need to be aware that solutions may require several attempts before working correctly.

SUMMARY

1 Starting social relationships involves being aware of, and then communicating those behaviours which let others see us in a positive light. This will involve teaching clients strategies to gather information and focus conversations on issues of mutual interest.

2 Deepening relationships involves slowly learning about others and disclosing in turn aspects about ourselves, beginning with rather superficial aspects and progressing tentatively to deeper, more personal issues.

3 Maintaining relationships involve recognising difficulties early and dealing with problems as they arise.

4 Clients should be taught the skill of behavioural specificity (remember the XYZ formula) and learn to watch for:

hidden agendas;
mind reading;
kitchen sinking;
sidetracking;
summarising self.

5 **Difficulties in a relationship should be viewed simply as a cue to solve inter-personal problems. Solving problems involves working towards a compromise solution. If either party tries to win unconditionally, the relationship loses.**

Chapter 10

Managing the thoughts that promote loneliness

Often the way clients think about events can promote loneliness. This chapter examines these thoughts in two parts. The first part focuses on thinking styles that can serve to trigger and maintain loneliness; the second on the thoughts that prevent clients from confronting their loneliness.

1 MANAGING THE THOUGHTS THAT CAUSE/MAINTAIN LONELINESS

Let us review briefly how people come to label themselves as lonely. The essence of this judgement seems to involve observing others, making assumptions about their social environment, and from this, setting up a standard or social norm which we then use to compare their social environments with our own. On the basis of these norms we make judgements about whether or not we are lonely. This is partly the reason why more people report feeling lonely over Christmas and New Year. If, for instance, they assume that most other people are out enjoying themselves with friends whilst they're in watching television, this comparison (based only on assumptions and assumed social norms) leads them to feel lonely. Social and group norms of this type are extremely complex, and leave ample room for inaccuracies. It is crucial, therefore, in dealing with clients where loneliness is adding to their difficulties, to help them understand, work through, and later challenge the thinking errors and distortions that contribute to feelings of loneliness. The majority of people believe that their own perception of the world is accurate, and therefore would be shared by others. Rather than considering that their loneliness could be a consequence of misinterpretation, they are convinced that the cause is external. For instance, I feel lonely because:

the people I do meet are odd;
the people I'd like to meet aren't interested in me;
it's because of where I live.

Alternatively, they see the problem as resulting from basic inadequacies in themselves:

I'm just odd;
I don't know what to say to people any more.

The counsellor, therefore, needs to convey to the client that there is no single way of correctly perceiving the world. Each person's perception of reality is merely a sample, restricted by the way their sensory systems access and interpret information. It follows, therefore, that the client's view of what is causing their difficulties may be inaccurate. Consequently, the challenge of helping the client begins with leading them to accept that there may be alternative ways of looking at their world. There are several methods available to the counsellor which, by encouraging the client to examine their thoughts, can reduce feelings of loneliness. Below are some of the more basic methods.

Catching thoughts

Clients are usually acutely aware of their feelings and emotions but pay little attention to the thoughts that prompted them. They can learn to gain awareness of their thoughts through a technique called 'thought catching' (Beck 1979). With this method, the counsellor invites the client to disclose a few thoughts on issues/events that are currently a concern for them. These are then noted down on a board or large piece of paper and used as visual triggers to probe for less obvious thoughts, and for the behaviours/feelings these thoughts lead to. For example:

Client discloses thoughts:	'I felt lonely at work today.'
Counsellor probes for thoughts:	'What were you thinking about when you felt lonely?'
Client answers either:	(a) by verbalising a series of thoughts; or (b) by saying 'I don't know'.

If the client is unable to identify upsetting thoughts about situations that were difficult for them, the following guidelines may help:

1 *Note down the EVENT*: Felt lonely at work.

2 *Achieve greater specificity*: Felt lonely after hearing colleagues planning to go to the pub.

3 *Identify REACTION*: Client felt sad.

4 *Identify the THOUGHT that caused the REACTION*: 'They won't ask me to join them . . . they don't like me.'

5 *Identify related actions*: Client pretends to be busy to avoid letting others know that he wants to join them.

Reviewing the event and the client's reaction to the event can help the client gain more insight into their thoughts. The client may be faced with thoughts that are indeed accurate, however they can never be certain because they avoided finding out. The counsellor, therefore, must help the client to discover whether or not they have got themselves into the habit of making incorrect judgements based on faulty assumptions with minimal evidence. To achieve this, the counsellor must encourage the client systematically to analyse his thoughts. The following section provides brief guidelines on promoting accurate thought analysis.

Thought analysis

We usually view ourselves as entirely rational beings, which can unfortunately stop us from acknowledging that at times we all think about things in a way that isn't entirely rational. We are most at risk of thinking in maladaptive ways when we feel unsure about ourselves. At such times we can develop rigid thought patterns which we assume are correct, and therefore do not attempt to alter.

Analysing thoughts involves recognising the distinction between irrefutable facts, and thoughts that have yet to be validated. This is not an easy matter; self-critical, demeaning, and maladaptive thoughts responsible for the client's distress can only be identified through careful exploratory discussion. Having achieved this, the maladaptive thoughts must be confronted and modified by using the following techniques.

Confronting thoughts – a skills compendium

Once maladaptive thoughts have been identified, the client must try to treat them simply as pieces of information which need to be validated before they can be accepted. In other words, each thought is merely a hypothesis to be tested and not a fact.

A useful method for both identifying and confronting maladaptive thoughts is to use a thought diary. Encourage the client to establish a habit of writing their thoughts down regularly. Then, taking each thought in turn, work collaboratively to challenge them with the following questions.

What evidence supports the thought?
What evidence contradicts it?
Do the facts of the situation support the thoughts?
Is there sufficient information to support this thought?
Where is the logic in the thought?
Would most people come to a similar conclusion given the same facts?

Urge clients to use this questioning whenever they recognise a possible maladaptive thought (as a rule of thumb, any thought that they find upsetting may be maladaptive). In addition it is useful to make them aware of the following common thinking errors so that they can confront the thoughts more efficiently.

1 *Selective attention.* Tendency to focus mostly on the negative or irrelevant aspects of situations.
2 *Confusing probabilities.* Tendency to worry about things that have little real chance of occurring.
3 *Extreme thinking.* Thinking in 'black and white' terms only, when in reality we deal also with shades of grey.
4 *Over-generalising.* Drawing broad conclusions from specific, often isolated events and minimal information.
5 *Distorting* the significance of events: Exaggerating or minimising the importance of events.
6 *Personification.* The belief we are the centre of all events, and hence, that other people must be looking at us and are acutely aware of our behaviour.
7 *Predicting the future.* Basing decisions on events which have yet to occur (and may never happen).

8 *Mindreading*. Responding to people in terms of what you think they are thinking.

After thinking errors have been identified, the counsellor can help the client to consider alternative ways of looking at the situation. For some clients, however, disputing their thought errors is not sufficient to convince them that they are inaccurate. In these cases, it may be necessary to expose the client to experiences powerful enough to change their misconceptions. For example:

Event: Forthcoming Xmas Party
Client's thoughts:
'I will not enjoy it.'
'No one will talk to me.'
'I'll feel stupid and leave early.'

Counsellor challenges these thoughts. If the client does not feel convinced the counsellor should encourage the client to expose themselves to a situation which could test these assumptions.

Counsellor: OK, how could we test out these thoughts to see if you're correct?

Client and counsellor negotiate a homework assignment as a behavioural experiment. For example:

Chosen situation: Going to another party and 'chatting' to at least one person there.
Preparation: Use relaxation techniques before going to the party. Prepare openings for conversation.
Expectations: As above, that he would not enjoy it, that no one would talk to him, and that he would feel stupid.
Evaluation: Didn't really enjoy it, BUT people did talk to me so the first thought I had was correct, but I did talk to people and did not feel stupid.

In designing such experiments, it is important to bear the following points in mind:

the goal of the experiment must be observable and specific;
it should be achievable (though not necessarily easy);
before beginning the 'test' the client must say what they expect to occur;

the test must be evaluated after completion in terms of initial predictions and an accuracy chart kept to give an indication of how accurate the initial expectations were.

Dilemmas, snags, and traps

Often counsellors become aware of consistent themes which seem to 'get in the way' of the client's progress. Ryle (1979) has listed several such factors and called them dilemmas, snags, and traps.

Dilemmas: can be expressed in two forms. The first is false dichotomies (the either/or scenario). An example of this is the common attitude that 'with friends I feel either too close, or too distant and lonely'. In such cases, the client seems to feel that there are always only the two extremes with no middle ground. This dichotomy often occurs because the client oscillates between emotional closeness, which can provoke fears of loss (e.g. if I get close, they may leave me; then I'll feel hurt), and emotional distance (which leaves them without the fear of loss, but also lonely).

The second is in terms of false assumptions (the if/then scenario). An example of this is 'if I'm intellectual then I have to be cold'. Here two constructs (cold and intellectual) are linked spuriously in the same way that 'fat' and 'jolly' are sometimes linked.

Traps are belief patterns which result in a person acting in ways that serve to confirm the negative belief (e.g. through circular reasoning):

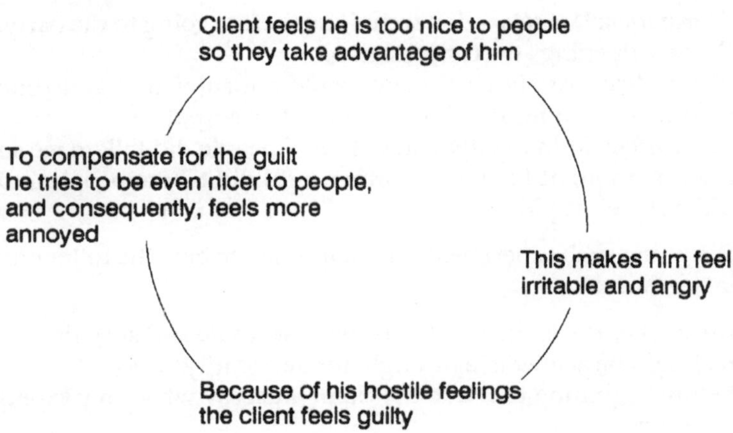

Snags refer to obstacles which are based on the anticipated consequences of action. The anticipations cause the client to suppress their desire to act. For instance, 'I let people push me around because nobody would like me if I stood up for myself'. These themes allow clients some justification for continuing to behave in maladaptive ways. The task of the counsellor here, is to be aware of these obstacles so that they can be worked through and challenged.

2 MANAGING THE THOUGHTS THAT UNDERMINE CLIENTS' ABILITIES TO OVERCOME LONELINESS

In the first part of this chapter we discussed the thoughts that trigger feelings of loneliness and the themes that serve to maintain it. Confronting these thinking patterns can lead the client to a decision to attempt change. However, in some cases, the change may involve interacting in a fashion that they have been avoiding for some time; consequently, they feel frightened. If people feel worried in this way, inhibitory anxiety results which can block the skills required for competent social interaction. Helping the client manage inhibitory anxiety involves confronting their perception of vulnerability. The feelings, thoughts, and actions that occur as a result of inhibitory anxiety are often so frightening for the client that they serve to reinforce feelings that change is impossible. It is extremely important to provide the client with a framework for understanding what they are experiencing.

Understanding inhibitory anxiety

Clients usually come to their counselling sessions fully able to interact appropriately, and can discuss their difficulties without questioning their ability to interact. However, if we change the context to meeting someone with whom they would like to begin a friendship, they suddenly find themselves at risk of being rejected, or of 'messing-up'. This causes them to enter what Beck and Emery (1985) have called vulnerability mode. This occurs when a person feels themselves subject to dangers over which they have minimal control. Positive information is ignored and the individual focuses on negative aspects of the situation and creates further obstacles by concentrating on their weaknesses and ignoring their strengths. This leads to excessive self-questioning and self-doubt, which in turn, generates further anxiety and even panic.

Anxiety is part of a primitive survival mechanism. Imagine, for instance, our primitive ancestors suddenly being confronted by a dangerous animal. Whatever they were doing would be stopped, and all biological and psychological systems would be switched to defensive mode (i.e. alert, tense, and ready to run/fight). This self-protection mechanism still operates today whenever we are faced with fearful situations, and can generate faintness, dizziness, and weakness. Consider, for instance, walking in a straight line without deviating more than a foot either way; it doesn't sound too difficult. However, consider the challenge of not diverging more than a foot either way on a flimsy bridge suspended at great height. The self-protection mechanisms discussed above would be activated (with all the accompanying bodily sensations, and self-doubts) and would make the task extremely difficult. Experienced construction workers, however, have learned to stop judging similar tasks as threatening or beyond their competence and are therefore not troubled by anxiety in these situations.

These same responses are also prominent in difficult social situations when the client is anticipating a problem. Anticipating problems activate a defence response just as if the feared problem was actually occurring. Helping the client to cope with this anticipatory anxiety first involves explaining to them how the above outline applies in their situation. Following this, the anxiety and arousal needs to be managed. We will discuss how to do this in the following sections.

Judging the reality of the threat

The key issue here is that to overcome loneliness, clients will probably need to confront social situations that they judge as both threatening, and beyond their competence. These judgements are usually replete with thinking errors that exacerbate feelings of vulnerability and disrupt inter-personal skills further. We therefore need to offer clients skills which will allow them to make more accurate judgements of threat.

Judging whether a situation will have negative consequences for self-esteem seems to be guided and corrupted by the nature of the client's thoughts and feelings about that situation. Typically these include:

> expectations of being disapproved of and criticised by others;
> feeling less able than others would in similar situations;
> feelings of being watched and judged by others;
> expecting the worst;
> feeling unable to adapt behaviour to changing circumstances;
> excessive thinking about bodily sensations related to embarrassment or anxiety.

Each of these issues can be reduced to a core thought which can be worked on further. For instance:

> *Thought*: 'I want to leave the coffee room, but cannot because I have only just come in'.

In this form, the thought is too vague to be tested for validity. The counsellor must help the client break it down into the core thoughts of which it is comprised:

> *Core thoughts*:
> People in the coffee room may think that I'm odd.
> They may think that I am leaving because I do not like them.
> They may have critical or bad thoughts about me.

These thoughts can then be challenged using the framework provided in part 1 of this chapter.

Enhancing coping capability

The client must be helped to cope with the symptoms of anxiety. A major feature of anxiety in social situations relates to the anticipation of being nervous prior to actually entering the situation. In addition the client may feel at risk of being overwhelmed by the anxiety, which is beyond their control. The expectation of a negative outcome tends to make the person more defensive, nervous and inhibited upon entering the situation. Relaxation techniques offer a useful starting point here, and are often a first taste of mastery over symptoms. Clients should be urged to set aside a regular slot each day to practise relaxation. They should find a quiet, comfortable place where they won't be interrupted, loosen any tight clothing and use the following procedures.

Controlled breathing

Close your eyes, place your hands at your sides and try to completely surrender your body to the chair/floor/bed. Let your shoulders fall, your jaw drop open slightly, and focus on your breathing. Just watch yourself breathe. After a minute or so, allow your breathing to slow down.

Focus on your abdomen, not your chest. To practise this, place a hand on top of your stomach and FEEL IT MOVE UP AS YOU BREATHE IN SLOWLY AND DOWN AS YOU BREATHE OUT. After a bit of practice you will be able to breathe in this fashion without watching your hand.

Regulate your breathing. Slowly breathe in to the count of four. Then breathe out slowly to the count of four. After you have the timing right say R–E–L–A–X to yourself each time you slowly breathe out. Practice this process for about five minutes. It's all right to check your watch, but do not set an alarm.

Relaxing the body

Next try relaxing your whole body by contracting and relaxing various muscle groups starting at your head and working down in the following way.

Tense up a muscle group as you breathe in and focus on this tension for three to five seconds. Then relax the muscle group as you breathe out. Notice the difference between the tension and relaxation, and focus on the feelings of relaxation you've created for about ten seconds.

Use this routine to work through the muscle groups listed below (one at a time). Tense each muscle group to about three-quarters tight. If you feel any discomfort omit that muscle group. Try to imagine tension draining away with each breathe out.

Face – Clench your jaw, frown and screw up your eyes tightly.

Neck – Tense your neck muscles.

Shoulders – Hunch your shoulders so that they almost touch your ears.

Arms – Make a muscle and clench both fists.

Stomach – Pull your stomach in so that you look as thin as possible.

Thigh – Straighten your knees and make your legs stiff.

Feet – Turn your toes up and try to point them towards your face.

The above procedures should be practised by the client daily and should take about twenty minutes each time to complete. Once mastered (usually within two weeks), it will allow them to achieve deep relaxation quickly and easily.

The client also needs to learn that they have the necessary skills to cope with difficult social situations. A knowledge of the skills and the norms of social relationships (Chapter 8) coupled with extensive practice can balance self-doubts and lead the client to a more realistic self-appraisal and greater self-confidence. Ideally, the skills repertoire should be as extensive as possible so that the client can choose the skill that they feel will work best for them in particular situations. Think of it as a 'tool box' of skills from which the client has a choice of 'tools'. As a rule of thumb, skills training should be approached in a graded fashion, beginning with easy problems, and working up to the more difficult ones. This enables the client to build up confidence in their coping skills before tackling difficult social situations.

Skill compendium

Below are outlined several skills which can be used by clients to increase their feelings of mastery of social situations.

Thought switching and distraction

If worrying thoughts begin to intrude during a social interaction, it is often too difficult to challenge them adequately at the time. What the client needs here, therefore, is a set of skills that they can use to block unwanted thoughts. The following techniques are based on the fact that people can only focus attention on one thing at a time. Suggest to the client that they try each of the techniques listed below and select the technique/s that they find most effective.

Count backwards from one hundred in threes (100,97,94, . . .).
Describe in detail an object in the room (what it's made of, how it was made, what it would cost).

Name every item you can see in the room.
Think of your favourite dish – describe how to make it from basic ingredients.
Decide on a scene which is relaxing and well known to you. Concentrate on it for as long as you can, trying to get in touch with the sights, smells, and feelings, as well as the image.

Visual imagery

People who find social situations difficult often carry around a distorted and inappropriate image of what the forthcoming interaction will be like. These images can trigger maladaptive thoughts. Induced imagery can have a positive effect on future skilled performance. For instance, we all have an image of how we would like to behave ideally. The client could benefit from developing an image of how they would like to behave in each difficult situation. This helps develop a sequence of images based on their knowledge of appropriate social behaviour. They can then practice scenarios within their imaginations before attempting the real events.

Self talk

Clients need to learn to replace habitual and maladaptive self-statements with coping statements. Conceptually these should have a message of mastery (e.g. self-statements like 'I'm doing OK', or 'I can handle this' instead of 'I don't believe this is happening to me'). In addition, unrealistic messages that contain imperatives like 'I should be perfect' or 'I should be coping better than this', increase the feeling of failure by setting unreasonable standards.

Clients should be taught to monitor their self-talk (i.e. what they say to themselves in their thoughts), and avoid statements like:

I must	...	instead use	...	would like.
Everyone	...	instead use	...	some people.
Everything	...	instead use	...	some things.
Nothing	...	instead use	...	not much.
Never	...	instead use	...	rarely.

SUMMARY

1 Thoughts can either trigger feelings of loneliness or prevent clients from confronting appropriately the social situations that could serve to ease loneliness.

2 People use assumptions about social norms to make judgements about their social environments. These judgements are fundamental to subsequent appraisals of whether or not they feel lonely.

3 Clients need to accept that there may be alternative ways of viewing the world. Consequently, their interpretation of their difficulties may not be entirely accurate.

4 The counsellor needs to help clients become aware of maladaptive thoughts, and teach techniques to confront and challenge these thoughts, and concomitant thinking errors.

5 The counsellor also needs to help clients enhance their coping capabilities by teaching a compendium of skills that they can later use in difficult inter-personal situations.

Appendix 1

Developing the MSW loneliness scale

The following pages detail the development of a loneliness test which has been constructed specifically to suit the social requirements of British subjects. In order to generate items for inclusion in the test, it was first necessary to determine which social resources are relevant to the British culture. Documented below are details of two studies by which this was achieved.

THE MAJOR SOCIAL RESOURCES USED BY THE BRITISH PUBLIC

Every type of relationship (friend, spouse, employer, colleague) is likely to provide a unique source for some social resources. However, it would clearly be impracticable to give due consideration to them all. Therefore, the studies considered the following fives relationships as being the major sources of important interaction: friends; intimate partners (sexual relationships, spouse, etc.); children; parents; and siblings. It was decided to restrict the age of the sample to between eighteen years and sixty-five years (inclusive). This was done to give some consideration to observations that the preferred interactions of adolescent, adult, and elderly people were likely to differ. For example, adult norms have been found to emphasise the development of the family and career (Dickets and Perlman 1981), whereas teenagers were more concerned with developing their own abilities (Kon 1981). Such differences would clearly affect the social resources each of these would desire; they should therefore be distinguished. The present classification of resources, therefore, is only relevant to British people between the ages of eighteen and sixty-five years.

In order to avoid assumptions about which interactions would be negative, respondents were simply asked to provide a list of interactions which were important to their satisfaction with their relationships (i.e. they may be important because they are undesirable and unwanted, or because they were desirable). The study identified over 2200 such interactions (Murphy *et al.* 1989), which were subsequently compiled into 406 distinct types of interaction. However, this was too large a number to include in a loneliness test (406 questions would pose a daunting task to any respondent). Therefore, in order to include only items which were important to most people (i.e. excluding items whose value was peculiar to only a few of the people studied), the 406 items were re-submitted to a new sample who were asked to place them in order of important (Murphy *et al.* 1989). On the basis of this, those items which were consistently important were selected and have been given in Table 1 in Chapter 3.

These items represent only a limited view of the preferred social resources of the British public because items about which there were inter-personal differences were removed during the second of the two studies. Nevertheless, as was discussed earlier, this limitation is necessary if the subsequent loneliness test is to be flexible enough to be used across different people within the culture.

There were no major sex differences among these items, neither was there a difference in the items considered important by psychiatric patients and non-patients. Nevertheless, in the first study, non-patients seemed to generate considerably more items than patients (45 per cent of all items generated were produced solely by non-patients, compared to a mere 4 per cent solely by patients). This difference was lost once patients were presented with all of the items (in the second of the two studies), which clearly suggests that although the resources they need do not differ (Study 2), patients find it difficult to list on command the resources they find helpful (Study 1). Presumably, this is either a result of their personal problems interfering with their thinking, or simply that they have too much on their mind already. Nevertheless, it is clear that attempting to produce a list of major social resources by simply asking such patients (as Henderson and his colleagues (1981) tended to do) is likely to produce an impoverished list. It is essential, therefore, that the general public is included at this stage.

By way of a brief note on the nature of some of the items identified here, it is interesting to observe that some of them were not interactions themselves, but concerned the health, honesty, and overall moral attitude of relationship members (for example, items 5, 6, 8, 18, 25 and 40). This indicates that as well as having needs for specific social resources, respondents also had more general needs concerning the styles of behaviour with which social resources are characterised.

The items identified by the above studies also provided material for continuing the discussion in Chapter 2 on the issue of the respective importance, when measuring loneliness, of close and casual relationships, and more generally close and casual interaction. Some investigators had tried to deal with the former question, of whether close relationships were more important than casual relationships, by embracing them both equally in their tests. For example, Russell *et al.* (1978) made general statements, in his UCLA loneliness scale, which avoided the issue by not specifying any particular type of relationship at all (see Table 2). Other investigators had addressed more directly the latter question of close and casual interaction, assuming that within all relationships it was close, intimate interactions which were of major importance (Henderson *et al.* 1981). In view of the information available to them, these represent fair attempts to accommodate the close/casual debate. However, the results of our two studies above suggested that their strategies had not been successful. For instance, considering first the relative importance of the various types of relationship. Table 1 shows that of the five relationship categories considered, interactions with intimate partner and child (generally relationships from the family unit) occurred most frequently (over 75) in the list, with friendship being mentioned considerably less often. Clearly, therefore, respondents' main concerns were with relatively close types of relationship. In view of this, general questions such as Russell *et al.*'s 'I feel shut out and excluded by others' (Table 2; Chapter 3) may generate misleading responses. For instance, a person might not feel excluded by most people at all, and would therefore answer the question with 'no', or 'rarely'. However, they may well feel excluded and rejected by a specific person with whom they have held a close relationship (perhaps a spouse has left them). Consequently, although having to answer Russell's general question with 'no/rarely', they might actually be feeling very shut out and lonely indeed.

Let us consider now, the relative frequency of close and casual interactions people require within their relationships (as pointed out above, Henderson excluded casual components of interaction as being unimportant). A problem in investigating this issue is that it is not easy to define what is exclusively a close (or casual) interaction. Of course, some interactions are by their nature intimate, such as sexual intercourse, but the list given in Table 1 includes very few items of this type. However, there are many interactions which are not necessarily intimate in themselves, but facilitate intimacy (such as when one provides help to another person). Categorising close interactions of the former type is not problematic because social convention usually dictates quite clearly what is and is not intimate. For example, the appropriate physical distance to maintain from people with whom one is not intimate is strongly regulated by social norms, and standing too close would often be seen as an intimate advance (Hall 1966). However, determining which interactions should be placed in the latter category is extremely problematic. To a large extent, this is because specific interactions do not consistently facilitate closeness. For example, Walster and Walster (1978) have shown that goal frustration by others promotes closeness, but Lott and Lott (1965) also found that facilitation of goal achievement is necessary for closeness to develop.

The problem of classification is compounded further by the fact that most interactions could be construed as promoting closeness, because all interactions constitute social contact and (not surprisingly) this variable has also been shown to promote closeness (Berkowitz 1980, p. 244). However, some of the items listed in Table 1 can have relatively little to do with establishing closeness because they occur with similar frequency in all interactions and are not easily open to change from one relationship to another. For example, items 5, 6, 18, and 25 concern basic honesty and morality. These characteristics are a function of a person's personality (Piaget 1948; Freud 1961; Kohlberg 1963) and as such are expressed relatively consistently across a person's interaction with all people. Consequently, it is difficult to construe these as anything but casual components of interaction. Contrary, therefore, to Henderson *et al.*'s (1981) suggestions, some casual aspects of interaction seem to be highly important in providing adequate social resources, and it is only problems of definition which limit further examples to support this. It can be concluded, therefore, that although respondents' main concerns were with the interactions in their most intimate relationships, within these relationships both close and casual interactions have importance. Consequently, casual interactions should not be excluded from tests of loneliness.

THE MURPHY–SUMMERFIELD–WATSON (MWS) LONELINESS SCALE

The forty items listed in Table 1 (Chapter 3) represent those social resources with which British people tend to satisfy their secondary and primary needs. Many of them are not relevant to other cultures, and (as was discussed in Chapter 3), even highly similar cultures such as America exhibit major differences regarding these items. In this context, there are no loneliness tests currently available which are relevant to the British adult population. The present section, therefore, describes how the above forty items have been compiled to give such a test (the MSW loneliness scale).

Although the forty items have been shown to be important to all British respondents, it is unlikely that they will be equally important to them. In other words, it cannot be assumed that all British people will experience equal distress when encountering a similar lack of availability of each resource. Clearly, therefore, simply asking about perceived *availability* will not sensitively reflect the actual feelings of deprivation (or loneliness) experienced. Consequently, it is necessary to ask respondents how *adequate* they feel the resource provision is. In this manner, an indication can be obtained of how well each social resource is provided for in terms of the respondent's own unique threshold of need.

Among the forty items are some which undermine the satisfaction of social needs (and are therefore undesirable in interaction), and some which fulfil social needs and are, therefore, desirable in interaction. Clearly then, questions regarding the latter should assess whether the item occurs frequently enough in their interactions to satisfy them. And, conversely, whether items of the former type occur rarely enough to satisfy them. However, a problem here is that, as was discussed above, interactions are not always consistently positive or negative in this manner. Consequently, it is not possible to make any assumptions about whether a respondent is likely to prefer more or less of the interactions. In view of this, questions will simply ask whether they are *satisfied* with each of the interactions. Hence, if an item is currently perceived as positive by a respondent an indication of 'high satisfaction' will mean that the interaction is occurring satisfactorily often. Similarly, if the interaction is currently perceived as undesirable, then 'highly satisfied' will indicate that it is occurring satisfactorily rarely. In either case, it will be possible to ascertain the adequacy of their social environment without needing to make assumptions about their preferences.

The forty items were compiled into a single questionnaire of the form given in Figure 10 (the test shown does not include all of the items, but is the final version which has been modified, as discussed below, to comply with validation findings). Each of the items refer to a specific type of relationship: either with friends, parents, children, or intimate partner. Consequently, in order to accommodate both respondents who were, and those who were not, currently involved in a relevant relationship, an additional question was included for each item (which can be seen in sections 'A' and 'B' of Figure 10). This meant that there were effectively eighty items (2 x 40) being considered.

The validity and reliability of the resulting instrument was then investigated.

The validity and reliability of the MSW loneliness scale

Various aspects of validity were investigated. The analyses were based on a sample of thirty-nine British male adults and fifty-nine British female adults.

Content validity

The main concern here was whether any of the items were redundant (exclusion of such items would minimise the length of the test). In this context, the purpose of the questionnaire was to observe inter- and intra-personal variation in social-environmental-adequacy. Clearly, therefore, items which failed to contribute to this, by eliciting only negligible response differences across subjects, would be redundant and should be excluded. In this context, it had previously been observed that standard deviations of 17 per cent of the scale range could occur simply through error in judgement by the respondent (Murphy *et al.* 1989). In order to ensure that variances across subject's scores were not merely reflections of this error items were excluded from the questionnaire if they elicited a standard deviation of less than 25 per cent of the scale.

Of the eighty items involved, thirteen elicited standard deviations which were less than 25 per cent of the scale range. They were, therefore, excluded from further consideration.

Internal construct validity

This concerned whether responses exhibited appropriate inter-item independence. The sample size (N=69) and the number of remaining items (n=67) precluded any meaningful analysis of the factor structure of the instrument (Lawlis and Chatfield 1974). However, it was observed that the inter-item correlation of questions concerned with 'satisfaction at being childless' were very high (Table 3). Similarly, correlations among items referring to 'satisfaction with being friendless' were high. In this case only three subjects were involved. Nevertheless, all correlations in this condition were significant ($p < 0.05$). Correlations were much smaller, however, regarding 'satisfaction with not having any parents' and 'not having an intimate partner'. They were also much smaller for questions concerning relationships currently held by the respondent.

The high correlations observed among items referring to being without a friend, and also among those referring to being childless (Table 3) were not surprising. In both contexts respondents were unlikely to have had experience of such relationships. Consequently, they would have had only minimal opportunity to develop the specific expectations implied by these items, thereby promoting high inter-item correlations. For instance, people currently without a child would usually never have had one. Similarly, those who indicated that they were friendless were unlikely ever to have had significant friendships. Duck (1983) for example, reviewed evidence which suggested that the lack of friendship in adult life was caused by enduring problems (such as social skills and personality deficits), which would have inhibited friendship formation throughout earlier life.

Table 3 Correlations among items (from the MSW loneliness scale) which refer to similar types of relationship

	Average correlations among items referring to relationships currently held	*Average correlations among items referring to relationships currently not held*
Friends	$r_{\bar{x}}$ = 0.49 (N=66 subjects	$r_{\bar{x}}$ = 0.94 (N=3 subjects)
Offspring	$r_{\bar{x}}$ = 0.28 (N=40 subjects)	$r_{\bar{x}}$ = 0.72 (N=24 subjects)
Parents	$r_{\bar{x}}$ = 0.03 (N=58 subjects)	$r_{\bar{x}}$ = 0.05 (N=10 subjects)
Intimate partner	$r_{\bar{x}}$ = 0.32 (N=57 subjects)	$r_{\bar{x}}$ = 0.37 (N=12 subjects)

Consequently, friendless adults would not have had the opportunity to develop specific conceptions of what to expect from friendship. It was of course arguable that some respondents may have reported having no friends simply because they had recently moved to a new neighbourhood. Such respondents could clearly have had previous friends, therefore, undermining the above conclusion. Nevertheless, this would not constitute a sound criticism because such people were unlikely actually to report themselves as friendless. For example, the important characteristics of friendship (to British subjects) concerned dependability and loyalty (Figure 10; section G). These factors would clearly endure considerable periods of separation. Consequently, although having moved away, a respondent was likely to continue perceiving them as friends. Both the childless and the friendless, therefore, were always likely to have been so, and would, therefore, not have had opportunity to develop specific expectations about such relationships. In view of this, any desire they had for such relationships would manifest itself in terms of a single vague construct. This would promote, as observed, high correlations between reported feelings about specific aspects of the relationships. Unfortunately, these conclusions could not be confirmed because subjects could not be re-contacted.

For all remaining categories of item respondents were likely to have had ample opportunity to develop sophisticated expectations, which would explain why correlations in these categories were much smaller (Table 3). For example, respondents answering questions about relationships they currently held would clearly have had an opportunity to develop such specificity. Similarly, those respondents currently without parents would once have had at least a surrogate parent with whom to develop specific expectations. Finally, even subjects who had never had an intimate partner would have relatively sophisticated expectations of such a relationship, because adolescent development is preoccupied with discussing and specifying the requirements of such interactions. Consequently, although often misguided, people tend to have considerable expectations of this relationship.

The present response patterns therefore, were consistent with respondent's own specificity about their social requirements. In view of this, it was clearly unnecessary to retain the multiple questions regarding childlessness and friendlessness. They were, therefore, combined into single general questions for each of the two conditions (sections D and H; Figure 10). This reduced the number of items by a further nineteen to forty-eight questions. These constituted the final version of the MSW loneliness scale, which has been given in Figure 10.

Discriminant validity

Various factors had been identified by previous research as potential confounders of social-environmental assessment procedures. Henderson (1984) had pointed out how respondents' negative dispositions could influence responses by promoting negative response sets. Similarly, Borys and Perlman's (1985) suggestions above, emphasised how the sense of stigma implied by certain responses to social questionnaires could confound assessments.

To evaluate the extent of this confounding with the present questionnaire, discriminance with both negativism and need for approval was investigated. Furthermore, although we had controlled for the effects of age by considering only adults, there was still likely to be some variance in response due to age (Stephens *et al.* 1978). Additionally, sex (Reisman 1981) could also promote variance in responses. Consequently, these factors were also considered.

Negativism was measured both in terms of self-view and general outlook. The former was assessed using Rosenberg's (1965) self-esteem scale, and the latter using a brief four-item question-

Table 4 Correlation of discriminant measures with MSW loneliness scale scores (N=69)

Discriminant Measure	*Correlations (*p<0.05)*
Social desirability	0.12
Self-esteem	0.31*
Negative outlook	0.41*
Age	0.31*
Sex	–.13

naire generated by the authors. Finally, need for approval was measured using Crowne and Marlowe's (1960) social desirability scale.

Total scores for the MSW loneliness scale were evaluated (using the method described in Figure 10). Scores for each of the discriminant measures were recoded to comply with the 4–16 range of the MSW scale scores. This simply involved stratifying the various score ranges to four equal sections, each then being attributed with a value of 4, 8, 12, or 16. Unfortunately, this was not possible with the 'sex' variable because of its dichotomous nature. Therefore, it maintained its original scale range of 2.

Table 4 shows that, of the various discriminant measures, self-esteem, negative outlook, and age correlated significantly with the MSW scale.

To consider first the correlation with self-esteem, previous investigators had pointed out that negativism could directly influence supports. For instance, the negativism may cause people to invest less in forming relations because they expect negative outcomes (Sarason and Sarason 1982). Clearly, therefore, some correlation would be expected, which did not reflect Henderson's confounding response sets. In view of this, and because the variance explained was small, discriminance was considered adequate on this variable.

The observation of a significant correlation between age and MSW scale scores suggested that the present adult range of the test may be too coarse, and that social need differences did in fact occur within (as well as across) the three developmental stages (adolescent, adult, elderly). This possibility is acknowledged, and future research may suggest age related re-specification of the test. Nevertheless, this will have only a marginal influence on scores because this age factor only accounts for 9 per cent of the variance (Table 4).

Finally, the low correlation of MSW scale scores with social desirability ratings (Table 4) indicated that socially approved responses within the test had been minimised. This was further supported by the observation of an insignificant 'sex' correlation, because socially preferred responses would have promoted a difference in the scores of the sexes (Borys and Perlman 1985).

Reliability

There was no reason to anticipate that loneliness would be consistent over time, because the availability of social resources was not a constant. It was not possible, therefore, to determine the reliability of the test using test/re-test methods, so the split-half procedure was used. Alternate items were selected to constitute two questionnaires, and the correlation between them was $r=0.7$ ($p < 0.001$), indicating adequate reliability in the test.

Appendix 2

Brief description of support scales which focus on network characteristics*

Source (i.e. major citation of scale)	*Scale*
Andrews *et al.*, 1978	6-item scale
Andrews *et al.*, 1978	5-item scale concerned exclusively with churches and clubs
Lin *et al.*, 1979	9-item scale
Schaefer *et al.*, 1981	9-item scale including marital status as one item
Hussaini *et al.*, 1982	3 separate items
Cohen *et al.*, 1982	1 item, frequency of visits with friends and relatives
Cohen *et al.*, 1982	6-item scale
Kessler and Essex, 1982	9-item scale
Aneshensel and Stone, 1982	1 item, number of close relatives, friends
Eaton, 1978	7 separate items
Warheit, 1979	1 item, number of close relatives, friends
Williams *et al.*, 1981	9-item scale
Thoits, 1982	4 separate items
Henderson *et al.*, 1981	16-item scale: integration and perceived access

* (adapted from Kessler and McLeod 1984, p.226)

Appendix 3

Brief description of support scales which focus on specific experiences and relationships*

Source (i.e. major citation of scale)	*Scale*
Emotional support: presence of an intimate, perception that others care for you, hold you in esteem, and consider you a part of a network of mutual obligation.	
Schaefer *et al.*, 1981	4-item scale: each item a weighted count of the number of supporters enumerated in a network inventory
Husaini *et al.*, 1982	1-item: spouse being understanding
Kessler and Essex, 1982	3-item scale
Brown and Harris, 1978	Coded from open-ended interview data
Dean and Ensel, 1982	2-item scale: lack of close companion and too few close friends (items reverse coded)
Thoits, 1984	2-item scale: confidant and integration
Henderson *et al.*, 1981	8-item scale
Pearlin *et al.*, 1981	2-item scale
Perceived availability of support: emotional, tangible, informational, and some combination.	
Andrews *et al.*, 1978	5-item scale
Schaefer *et al.*, 1981	9-item scale: tangible only
Wilcox, 1981	Count of potential supporters

Continued

* (adapted from Kessler and McLeod 1984, p. 226–7)

Wilcox, 1981	18-item: 6 items each for emotional, tangible, and informational
Clearly and Mechanic, 1983	5-item scale
House and Wells, 1978	4 multi-item scales: for supervisor, co-worker, spouse, and other family and friends
LaRocco *et al.*, 1980	3 multi-item scales: for supervisor, co-worker, and family and friends
Warheit, 1979	2 separate items
Recent use of support.	
Schaefer *et al.*, 1981	1 item: frequency of recent use summed over all supporters* enumerated in a network inventory
Aneshensel and Stone, 1982	6-item scale
McFarlane *et al.*, 1983	6-item scale: each item created by averaging over all supporters enumerated in a network inventory
Adequacy of support	
Henderson *et al.*, 1981	12-item: intimacy
Henderson *et al.*, 1981	17-item: integration

*Supporters: Those who provide the social support.

References

Aagaard, J. (1984) Stressful life events and illness. In: Cullen J., Siegrist J., and Wegmann H. (eds) *Breakdown in human adaptation to stress (I)* Netherlands: Martinus Nijhoff Publishers pp. 98–122.

Altman, E. and Taylor, D. (1973) *Social penetration: Developing inter-personal relationships*. New York: Holt, Rinehart & Winston.

Andrews, G., Tennant, C., Hewson, D.M. and Vaillant, G.E. (1978) 'Life event stress, social support, coping style and risk of psychological impairment', *Journal of Nervous and Mental Diseases, 166*, 307–316.

Aneshensel, C.S. and Stone, J.D. (1982) Stress and depression: A test of the buffering model of social support *Archives of General Psychiatry, 39*, 1392–1396.

Anson, P.F. (1932) *The Quest of Solitude*, New York: E.P. Dutton & Co. Inc.

Antonucci, T. and Depner, C. (1982) Social support and informal helping relationships, In: T.A. Wills (ed.) *Basic Processes in Helping Relationships*, New York: Academic Press.

Argyle, M. (1969) *Social Interaction*. London: Methuen.

Asch, S.E. (1958) Effects of group pressures upon modification and distortion of judgements, In: E.E. Maccoby, T.M. Newcomb, and E.L. Hartley (eds) *Readings in Social Psychology*. New York: Holt, Rinehart & Winston (pp. 174–183).

Bandura, A. (1977) 'Self-efficacy: Toward a unifying theory of behavioural change', *Psychological Review 84*, 191–215.

Barrera, M. (1981) Social support in the adjustment of pregnant adolescents: Assessment issues. In: B.H. Gottlieb (ed.) *Social Networks and Social Support*, Beverly Hills, California: Sage.

Beck, A.T. and Emery, G. (1985) *Anxiety and Phobias: A cognitive approach*. New York: Basic Books.

—— (1979) *Cognitive therapy of anxiety and phobic disorders*. Philadelphia: Center for Cognitive Therapy.

Beck. A.T. and Young, J.E. (1978) 'College blues'. *Psychology Today*, September.

Bell, R.A. and Daly, J.A. (1984) *Affinity seeking: Its nature and correlates*. San Francisco: Paper presented to International Communication Association.

Berkman L.F. and Syme, S.L. (1979) 'Social networks, host resistance and mortality: A nine-year follow-up study of Alameda County residents'. *American Journal of Epidemiology, 109*, 186–204.

Berkowitz, L. (1980) *A survey of social psychology*, (2nd edn) New York: Holt, Rinehart & Winston.

Birley, J.C.T. and Brown, G.W. (1970) 'Crises and life changes preceding the onset or relapse of acute schizophrenia: Clinical aspects'. British Journal of Psychiatry, 116, 327–333.

Böll, H. (1967) *Irish Journal*, New York: McGraw-Hill.

Borys, S. and Perlman, D. (1985) 'Gender differences in loneliness', *Personality and Social Psychology Bulletin*, New York: Pergamon.

Bowlby, J. (1973) *Attachment and loss, Volume 2: Separation: Anxiety and Anger*, New York: Basic Books.

—— (1980) *Attachment and loss, Volume 3: Loss, sadness and depression*, London: The Hogarth Press.

Brehm, J.W. and Cohen, A.R. (1962) 'Explorations in cognitive dissonance, New York: Wiley.

Broadhead, W.E., Kaplan, H.H. and James, S.A. (1983) 'The epidemiologic evidence for a relationship between social support and health'. *American Journal of Epidemiology*, 117, 521–537.

Broom, L. and Selznick, P. (1973) *Sociology*, New York: Harper & Row.

Brown, G.W., Bhrolchain, M. and Harris, T. (1975) 'Social class and psychiatric disturbance among women in an urban population'. *Sociology 9*, 225–254.

Brown. G.W. and Birley, J.L. T. (1968) 'Crises and life changes and onset of schizophrenia'. *Journal of Health and Social Behaviour 9*, 203–214.

Brown, G.W. and Harris, T. (1978) *The Social origins of depression: A study of psychiatric disorder in women*, London: Tavistock Free Press.

Brown, R. (1986) *Social Psychology* (Second Edition). London: Collier Macmillan Publishers.

Cassel, J. (1974) 'Psychological processes and 'stress': Theoretical formulations'. *International Journal of Health Services, 4*, 471–482.

Cleary, P.D. and Mechanic, D. (1983) 'Sex differences in psychological distress among married women'. *Journal of Health and Social Behaviour, 24*, 300–314.

Cobb, S. (1976) 'Social support as a moderator of life stress'. *Psychosomatic Medicine, 38*, 300–341.

Cohen, P., Stuening, E.L., Muhlin, G.L., Genevie, L.E., Kaplan, S.R. and Peck, H.B. (1982) 'Community stressors, mediating conditions, and well-being in urban neighbourhoods', *Journal of Community Psychology, 10*, 377–391.

Cohen, S. and McKay, G. (1985) Social support, stress and the buffering hypothesis: A theoretical analysis. In: A. Baum, J.E. Singer and S.E. Taylor (eds) *Handbook of psychology and health, vol. 4*, Hillsdale: Erlbaum.

Cohen, S. and Syme, L. (eds) (1984) *Social support and health*, New York: Academic Press.

Cooley, C.H. (1909) *Social organisations: A study of the larger mind*. New York: C. Scribner's Sons (p. 23).

Coombs, R.H. (1969) 'Social participation, self-concept, and interpersonal valuation'. *Sociometry, 32*, 273–286.

Crowne, D.P. and Marlowe, D. (1960) 'A new scale of social desirability independent of psychopathology'. *Journal of Consulting Psychology, 24,* 349–354.

—— (1964) *The approval motive.* New York: Wiley.

Dean, A. and Ensel, W.M. (1982) 'Modelling social support, life events, competence and depression in the context of age and sex'. *Journal of Community Psychology, 10,* 392–408.

Deutsch, M. and Gerard, H.B. (1955) 'A study of normative and informational social influences upon individual judgement'. *Journal of Abnormal and Social Psychology, 51,* 629–636.

Dickens, W.J. and Perlman, D. (1981) Friendship over life cycle. In: S. Duck and R. Gilmour (eds) *Personal relationships 2: Developing personal relationships.* London: Academic Press.

Dittes, J.E. (1959) 'Attractiveness of a group as a function of self esteem and acceptance by group', *Journal of Abnormal and Social Psychology, 59,* 77–82.

Duck, S.W. (1982) A topography of relationship disengagement and dissolution. In: S.W. Duck (ed.) *Personal relationships 4: Dissolving personal relationships. London: Academic Press.*

Dunkel-Schetter, C. and Wortman, C. (1981) Dilemmas of social support: Parallels between victimization and aging. In: S.B. Kiesler, J.N. Morgan and V.K. Oppenheimer (eds) *Aging: Social change.* New York: Academic Press.

D'Zurilla, T.J. and Goldfried, M.R. (1971) 'Problem solving and behaviour modification'. *Journal of Abnormal Psychology, 78.* 107–126.

Eaton, W.W. (1978) 'Life events, social supports, and psychiatric symptoms: A re-analysis of the New Haven data'. *Journal of Health and Social Behaviour, 19,* 230–234.

Eliot, T.S. (1950) *The Cocktail Party.* New York: Harcourt Brace.

Fagin, L. (1981) *Unemployment and health in families.* London: DHSS.

Festinger, L. (1957) *A theory of cognitive dissonance.* Stanford, Cal.: Stanford University Press.

Fiore, J., Becker, J. and Coppel, D. (1983) 'Social network interactions: A buffer or a stress'. *American Journal of Community Psychology, 11,* 423–439.

Firestone, L.J., Kaplan, K.J. and Russell, J.C. (1973) 'Anxiety, fear, and affiliation with similar-state versus dissimilar-state others: Misery sometimes loves miserable company'. *Journal of Personality and Social Psychology, 26,* 409–414.

Fitz, D. and Gerstenzang, S. (1978) *Anger in everyday life: When, where and with whom.* St. Louis: University of Missouri (ERIC Document Reproduction Services No. ED 160 966).

Freud, S. (1961) The ego and the id. In: J. Strachey and A. Freud (Trans.) *The complete psychological works of Sigmund Freud, Volume 21.* London: Hogarth.

Gaertner, S.L. and Dovidio, J.F. (1977) 'The subtlety of white racism, arousal and helping behaviour', *Journal of Personality and Social Psychology, 35,* 691–707.

Garfield, S.L. and Bergin, A.E. (eds) (1978) *Handbook of psychotherapy and behaviour change.* New York: Wiley.

Gecas, V. (1971) 'Parental behaviour and dimensions of adolescent self-evaluation'. *Sociometry, 34*, 466.

Geer, J.H. and Jarmecky, L. (1973) 'The effects of being responsible for reducing another's pain on subject's response and arousal'. *Journal of Personality and Psychology, 26*, 232–237.

Gelles, R.J. and Strauss, M.A. (1979) 'Violence in the American family'. *Journal of Social Issues, 35*, 15–39.

Goldberg, E.L., Comstock, G.W. and Graves, C.G. (1980) 'Psychosocial factors and blood pressure'. *Psychological Medicine, 10*, 243–255.

Goldschmidt, S. (1975) 'Absent eyes and idle hands: Socialization for low effect among the Sebi'. *Ethos, 3*, 157–164.

Gottman, J.M. Notarius, C., Gonso, J. and Markman, H. (1976) *A couple's guide to communication*. Illinois: Research Press.

Hall, E.T. (1966) *The hidden dimension*. Garden City, New York: Doubleday.

Hawkins, N.F., Davies, R. and Holmes, T.H. (1957) 'Evidence of psychosocial factors in the development of pulmonary tuberculosis'. *American Review of Respiratory Disorders, 75*, 768–780.

Heider, F. (1944) 'Social perception and phenomenal causality'. *Psychological Review, 51*, 358–374.

Henderson, A.S. (1984) 'Interpreting the evidence on social support'. *Social Psychiatry, 19*, 49–52.

Henderson, A.S. and Moran, P.A. P. (1983) 'Social relationships during the onset and remission of neurotic symptoms: A prospective community study'. *British Journal of Psychiatry, 143*, 467–472.

Henderson, S., Byrne, D.G. and Duncan-Jones, P. (1981) *Neuroses and the social environment*. New York: Academic Press.

Henderson, S., Duncan-Jones, P., Mcauley, H. and Ritchie, K. (1978) 'The patient's primary group'. *British Journal of Psychiatry, 132*, 74–86.

Hilgard, E.R., Atkinson, R.L. and Atkinson, R.C. (1979) *Introduction to Psychology*. New York: Harcourt Brace & Jovanovich, Inc.

Hinkle, L.E. and Wolff, H.G. (1957) 'Health and social environment: Experimental investigations'. In: A.H. Leighton, J.A. Clausen and R.N. Wilson, (eds) *Explorations in social psychiatry*. New York: Basic Books.

—— (1958) 'Ecologic investigations of the relationship between illness, life experiences and the social invironment'. *Annals of Internal Medicine, 49*, 1373–1388.

Hirsch, B. (1980) 'Natural support systems and coping with major life changes'. *American Journal of Community Psychology, 8*, 159–172.

Holahan, C.L. and Moos, R.H. (1981) 'Social support and psychological distress: A longitudinal analysis'. *Journal of Abnormal Psychology, 90*, 365–370.

House, J.S. and Wells, J.A. (1978) 'Occupational stress, social support and health'. In: A. McLean, G. Black and M. Colligan (eds) *Reducing occupational stress: proceedings of a conference*. Washington DC: US Department of Health, Education and Welfare (NIOSH) – Publication No. 78–140.

Hussaini, B.A., Neff, J.A., Newbrough, J.R. and Moore, M.C. (1982) 'The stress buffering role of social support and personal competence among the rural married'. *Journal of Community Psychology, 10*, 409–426.

Israel, B.A. (1982) 'Social networks and health status: Linking theory research and practice'. *Patient Counsel Health Editorial, 4*, 65–79.
Jackson, C. (1978) Article in the *Wisconsin State Journal, Sept. 7*.
Jackson, P.R. and Warr, P.B. (1984) 'Unemployment and psychological ill-health'. *Psychological Medicine, 14*, 605–614.
Jacobs, S. and Myers, J. (1976) 'Recent life events and acute schizophrenic psychosis: A controlled study'. *Journal of Nervous and Mental Diseases, 162*, 75–87.
Jenkins, C.D. (1976) 'Recent evidence supporting psychologic and social risk factors for coronary diseases'. *New England Medical Journal, 294*, 987–994, 1033–1038.
Jenkins, R., Macdonald, A., Murray, J. and Strathdec, G. (1982) 'Minor psychiatric morbidity and the threat of redundancy in a professional group'. *Psychological Medicine, 12*, 799–807.
Jones, E.E. and Davis, K.E. (1965) 'A theory of correspondent inferences. From acts to dispositions: The attribution process in person perception'. In: L. Berkowitz (ed.) *Advances in experimental social psychology Vol. 2*. New York: Academic Press.
Jones, E.E. and Gerard, H.B. (1967) *Foundations of Social Psychology*, New York: Wiley.
Jones, E.E. and Nisbett, R.E. (1972) 'The actor and the observer: Divergent perceptions of the causes of behaviour'. In: E.E. Jones, D.E. Kanouse, H.H. Kelley, R.E. Nisbett, S. Valins and B. Weiner (eds) *Attribution: perceiving the causes of behaviour*. Morristown NJ: General Learning Press.
Jones, S.C. and Schneider, D.J. (1968) 'Certainty of self-appraisal and reactions to evaluations from others'. *Sociometry, 31*, 395–403.
Jong-Gierveld, J. de (1984) *Developing and testing a theory about loneliness*. Paper presented at the Second International Conference on Personal Relationships: University of Wisconsin, Madison, USA.
Kahn, R.L. and Antonucci, T.C. (1980) 'Convoys of social support: A life-course approach'. In: P.B. Baltes and D.G. Brim (eds) *Life-span development and behaviour*. New York: Academic Press.
Kaplan, B.H. (1975) 'An epilogue: Toward further research on family and health'. In:B. H. Kaplan and J.C. Cassell (eds) *Family and health: An epidemiological approach*. Chapel Hill: Institute for Research in Social Science, University of North Carolina.
Kelleher, M.J. (1972) 'Cross-national (Anglo-Irish) differences in obsessional symptoms and traits of personality'. *Psychological Medicine, 2*, 33–41.
Kelley, H.H. (1967) 'Attribution theory in social psychology. In: D. Levine (ed.) *Nebraska symposium on motivation*. Lincoln, Neb: University of Nebraska Press.
Kelley, H.H., Berscheid, E., Christensen, A., Harvey, J.H., Huston, T.L., Levinger, G., McClintock, E., Peplau, L.A. and Peterson, D.R. (1983) *Close relationships*. New York: W.H. Freeman and Co.
Kenny, D.A. (1973) 'Cross-lagged and synchronous common factors in panel data'. In: A.S. Goldberger and O.D. Duncan (eds) *Structural equation models in the social sciences*. New York: Seminar.

—— (1979) *Correlation and Causality*. New York: John Wiley & Sons.

Kessler, R.C. and Essex, M. (1982) 'Marital status and depression: The role of coping resources'. *Social Forces, 61*, 484–507.

Kessler, R.C. and Mcleod, J.D. (1984) 'Social support and mental health in community samples'. In: S. Cohen and S.L. Syme (eds) *Social support and health*. New York: Academic Press.

Kessler, R.C., Price, R.H. and Wortman, C.B. (1985) 'Social factors in psychopathology: Stress, social support, and coping processes'. *Annual Reviews of Psychology, 36*, 531–572.

Kohlberg, L. (1963) 'The development of children's orientations towards a moral order: 1. Sequence in the development of moral thought'. *Vita Humana, 6*, 11–33.

Kon, I.S. (1981) 'Adolescent friendship'. In: S. Duck, and R. Gilmour (eds) *Personal relationships 2: Developing personal relationships*. London: Academic Press (pp. 187–204).

Krebs, D.L. (1975) 'Empathy and altruism'. *Journal of Personality and Social Psychology, 32*, 1134–1146.

Langer, E.J. and Roth, J. (1975) 'Heads I win, tails it's a chance: The illusion of control as a function of the sequence of outcomes in a purely chance task'. *Journal of Personality and Social Psychology, 32*, 951–955.

LaRocco, J.M., House, J.S. and French, J.R.P. Jr (1980) 'Social support, occupational stress, and health'. *Journal of Health and Social Behaviour, 21*, 202–218.

Latané, B. and Darley, J.M. (1968) 'Group inhibition of bystander intervention in emergencies'. *Journal of Personality and Social Psychology, 10*, 215–221.

Latané, B. and Rodin, J. (1969) 'A lady in distress: Inhibiting effects of friends and strangers on bystander intervention'. *Journal of Experimental and Social Psychology*, 189–202.

Lawlis, D.N. and Chatfield, D. (1974) *Multivariate approaches for the behavioural sciences: A brief text*. Texas: Texas Technical University Press.

Leiberman, M. (1982) 'The effects of social supports on responses to stress'. In: L. Goldberg and S. Breznitz (eds) *Handbook of Stress*. New York: The Free Press.

Leibert, R.M. and Spiegler, M.D. (1974) *Personality: Strategies for the Study of Man*. Illinois: The Dorsey Press.

Levy, R.I. (1973) *Tahitians: Mind the experience in the society islands*. Chicago: University of Chicago Press.

Lin, N., Simeone, R., Ensel, W. and Kuo, W. (1979) 'Social support stressful life events, and illness: A model and an empirical test'. *Journal of Health and Social Behaviour, 20*, 108–119.

Little, K.B. (1968) 'Cultural variations in social schemata'. *Journal of Personality and Social Psychology, 10*, 1–7.

Little, R. (1964) 'Buddy relations in combat performance'. In: M. Janowitz (ed.) *The new military*. New York: Russel Sage.

Lott, A.J. and Lott, B.E. (1965) 'Group cohesiveness as interpersonal attraction: A review of relationships with antecedent and consequent variables'. *Psychological Bulletin, 64*, 259–309.

McFarlane, A.H., Norman, G.R., Streiner, D.L. and Roy, R.G. (1983) 'The process of social stress: Stable, reciprocal and mediating relationships'. *Journal of Health and Social Behaviour, 24*, 160–173.

McGill, D. and Pearce, J.K. (1982) British families. In: M. McGoldrick, J.K. Pearce and J. Giordano (eds) *Ethnicity and family therapy*. New York: The Guilford Press.

McGoldrick, M. (1982) Irish families. In: M. McGoldrick, J.K. Pearce and J. Giordano (eds) *Ethnicity and family therapy*. New York: The Guilford Press.

Maslow, A.H. (1954) *Motivation and personality*. New York: Harper & Row.

Mead, M. (1939) *From the south seas: Studies of adolescence and sex in primitive societies*. New York: William Morris.

Mehrabian, A. (1969) 'Significance of posture and position in the communication of attitude and status relationships'. *Psychological Bulletin, 71*, 359–372.

Meichenbaum, D. (1977) *Cognitive behaviour modification: an integrative approach*. New York: Plenum.

Midelfort, C.F. and Midelfort, H.C. (1982) Norwegian families. In: M. McGoldrick, J.K. Pearce and J. Giordano (eds) *Ethnicity and Family Therapy*. New York: The Guilford Press.

Midlarksy, E. and Bryan, J.H. (1967) 'Training charity in children'. *Journal of Personality and Social Psychology, 5*, 408–415.

Miller, P. McM. and Ingham, J.G. (1976) 'Friends, confidants and symptoms'. *Social Psychiatry, 11*, 51–58.

Money, J., Hampson, J.G. and Hampson, J.L. (1955) 'Hermaphroditism: Recommendations concerning assignment of sex, change of sex, and psychologic management'. *Bulletin Johns Hopkins Hospital, 97*, 284–300.

Moos, R.H. and Mitchell, R.E. (1982) 'Social network resources and adaptation: A conceptual framework'. In: T.A. Wills *Basic processes in helping relationships*. New York: Academic Press.

Moreno, J. (1934) *Who shall survive: A new approach to the problem of human interrelations*. Washington DC: Nervous and Mental Disease Publishing.

Murphy, A.E. (1987) 'Brent Borough Council – Counsellor for the long-term unemployed'. Personal Communication.

Murphy, P.M., Summerfield, A.B. and Watson, J.P. (1989) *Loneliness, Support and Social Needs: Universally or culturally defined?* Unpublished manuscript.

Nisbett, R.E., Caputo, C., Legant, P. and Marecek, J. (1973) 'Behaviour as seen by the actor and as seen by the observer'. *Journal of Personality and Social Psychology, 27*, 154–164.

Pavlov, I.P. (1927) *Conditioned reflexes*. New York: Oxford University Press.

Paykel, E.S., Myers, J.K., Dienelt, M.N., Klerman, G.L., Lindenth, J.J. and Pepper, M.P. (1969) 'Life events and depression'. *Archives of General Psychiatry, 21*, 753–760.

Pearlin, L.I., Lieberman, M.A., Menagham, E.G. and Mullan, J.T. (1981) 'The stress process'. *Journal of Health and Social Behaviour, 22*, 337–356.

Peplau, L.A. and Perlman, D. (1979) 'Blueprint for a social psychological theory of loneliness'. In: M. Cook and G. Wilson (eds) *Love and attraction: An international conference*. New York: Pergamon.

Peterson, D.R. (1983) 'Conflict'. In: H.H. Kelley, E. Berscheid, A. Christensen,

J.H. Harvey, T.L. Huston, G. Levinger, E. McClintock, L.A. Peplau and D.R. Peterson. *Close Relationships*. New York: W.H. Freeman and Co.

Piaget, J. (1948) *The moral judgement of children*. New York: International University Press.

Platt, S. and Kreitman, N. (1985) 'Parasuicide and unemployment among men in Edinburgh 1968–1982'. *Psychological Medicine, 15*, 113–124.

Rahe, R.H., Bennett, L., Ramon, M., Siltamen, P. and Arthur, R.J. (1973) 'Subjects' recent life changes and coronary heart disease in Finland', *American Journal of Psychiatry, 130*, 1222–1226.

Raphael, B. (1977) 'Preventive intervention with the recently bereaved'. *Archives and General Psychiatry, 34*, 1450–1454.

Reisman, J.M. (1981) In: S. Duck and R. Gilmour (eds) *Personal relationships 2: Developing personal relationships*. London: Academic Press.

Rook, K.S. (1984) 'Research on social support, loneliness, and social isolation'. In: P. Shaver (ed.) *Review of personality and social psychology*. Beverly Hills: Sage Publications.

Rosenberg, M. (1965) *Society and the adolescent self image*. Princeton: Princeton University Press.

Rosenblatt, P.C. (1977) 'Needed research in commitment in marriage'. In: G. Levinger and H.L. Raush (eds) *Close Relationships: Perspectives in the meaning of intimacy*. Massachusetts: University of Massachusetts Press.

Rusbult, C.E. (1980) 'Commitment and satisfaction in romantic associations: A test of the investment model'. *Journal of Experimental Social Psychology, 16*, 172–186.

Russell, D., Peplau, L.A. and Ferguson, M.L. (1978) 'Developing a measure of loneliness'. *Journal of Personality Assessment, 42*, 290–294.

Rutter, M. (1972) *Maternal deprivation reassessd*. Middlesex: Penguin Books Ltd (p. 110).

Ryle, A. (1979) 'The focus in brief interpretive psychotherapy: Dilemmas, traps, and snags, as target problems'. *British Journal of Psychiatry, 134*, 46–54.

Sarason, I.G. and Sarason, B.R. (1982) 'Concommitants of social support: Attitudes, personality characteristics, and life experiences'. *Journal of Personality, 50*, 331–344.

Schachter, S. (1959) *The psychology of affiliation*. Stanford, Cal.: Stanford University Press.

Schaefer, C., Coyne, J. and Lazarus, R. (1981) 'Health related functions of social support'. *Journal of Behavioural Medicine, 4*, 381–406.

Schaffer, R. (1980) *Mothering*. Somerset: Fontana/Open Books.

Sisenwein, R.J. (1964) *Loneliness and the individual as viewed by himself and others*. Doctoral Dissertation. Columbia University: University Microfilm Np 65–4768.

Sokolovsky, J., Cohen, C., Berger, D. and Geiger, J. (1978) 'Personal networks of ex-mental patients in a Manhattan SRO hotel'. *Human Organisations, 37*, 5–15.

Solomon, G.F. (1969) 'Emotions, stress, the central nervous system, and immunity'. *Annual New York Academy of Science, 164*, 335–343.

Somer, R. (1969) *Personal space*. Englewood Cliffs NJ: Prentice-Hall Inc. (p. 65).

Stephens, R.C., Blau, Z.S. and Oser, G.T. (1978) 'Aging social support systems, and social policy'. *Journal of Gerontology and Social Work, 1*, 33–45.

Stoller, R. (1968) *Sex and Gender*. New York: Science House.
Straus, M.A. and Hotalling, G.T. (eds) (1980) *The social causes of husband-wife violence*. Minneapolis: Univeristy of Minnesota Press.
Surtees, P. (1984) 'Kith, kin and psychiatric health: A Scottish survey'. A paper presented to the VIIth World Congress of Psychiatry, Vienna. In A.S. Henderson 'Interpreting the evidence on social support'. *Social Psychiatry, 19*, 49–52.
Sykes, J.B. (1982) *The Concise Oxford Dictionary of Current English*. (Seventh Edition). Oxford: Oxford University Press.
Tennant, C. and Bebbington, P. (1978) 'The social causation of depression: A critique of the work of Brown and his colleagues'. *Psychological Medicine, 8*, 565–575.
Thoits, P.A. (1982) 'Conceptual, methodological, and theoretical problems in studying social support as a buffer against life stress'. *Journal of Health and Social Behaviour, 23*, 145–159.
—— (1984) 'Explaining distributions of psychological vulnerability – Lack of social support in the face of life stress'. *Social Forces, 63*, 453–481.
Thomas, J. and Weiner, E.A. (1974) 'Psychological differences among groups of critically ill hospitalised patients, non-critical ill hospitalised patients and well controls'. *Journal of Clinical Psychology, 42*, 274–279.
Times, The (1983) *Sunday Times* article, *Loneliness*, November.
Walster, E. and Walster, G.W. (1978) *A new look at love*, Reading, Mass.
Warheit, G.J. (1979) 'Life events, coping, stress and depressive symptomatology'. *American Journal of Psychiatry, 136*, 502–507.
Weiss, R.S. (ed.) (1973) *Loneliness: The experience of emotional and social isolation*. Cambridge, Mass.: MIT Press.
—— (1974) 'The provisions of social relationships'. In: Z. Rubin (ed.) *Doing Unto Others*. Englewood Cliffs, New Jersey: Prentice Hall.
—— (1975) *Marital Separation*. New York: Basic Books.
—— (1979) *Going it alone: The family life and social situation of the single parent*. New York: Basic Books.
Wellman, B. (1979) 'The community question: The intimate networks of East Yorkers'. *American Journal of Sociology, 84*, 1201–1231.
Wicklund, R.A. and Brehm, J.W. (1976) *Perspectives on cognitive dissonance*. Hillsdale NJ: Erlbaum.
Wilcox, B.L. (1981) 'Social support, life stress, and psychological adjustment: A test of the buffering hypothesis'. *American Journal of Community Psychology, 9*, 371–386.
Williams, A.W., Ware, J.E. and Donald, C.A. (1981) 'A model of mental health, life events and social supports applicable to general populations'. *Journal of Health and Social Behaviour, 22*, 324–336.
Wortman, C.B. (1975) 'Some determinants of perceived control'. *Journal of Personality and Social Psychology, 31*, 282–294.
—— (1984) 'Social support and the cancer patient: Conceptual and methodological issues'. *Cancer, 53*, 2339–2360.
Zborowski, M. (1969) *People in pain*. San Francisco: Jossey-Bass.
Zola, I.K. (1966) 'Culture and symptoms: An analysis of patients' presenting complaints'. *American Sociological Review, 5*, 141–155.

Index